The Moscow Kremlin's museums are open daily, except Thursdays, from 10 a. m. to 5 p. m. The ticket-offices are located in the Alexandrov Gardens at the Troitskiy Bridge. An entry ticket provides visitors admission to all the Kremlin's museums, except for the Armory Chamber, the Diamond Fund exposition and the Kremlin's Large Palace):

- the Assumption Cathedral;
- the Annunciation Cathedral;
- the Archangel's Cathedral;
- the Church of Laying Our Lady's Holy Robe;
- the Museum of the 17th Century Russian Applied Art and Private Life at the Patriarch's Palace.

You can also buy a permit for taking pictures inside the museums.

Access to the Kremlin is via the Borovitskiye Gate and the Troitskiye Gate. Large shopping bags, briefcases and rucksacks must be left in the cloakroom before entering the Kremlin's territory. The cloakroom is located in the Alexandrov Gardens, near the Kutafiya Tower.

You can order a private excursion at the Excursion Office located at: 3/4 [illegible] fer to be on your own, you can borrow a portable player with a pre-recorded explanation in Russian, English, French, German, Italian or Spanish. In the Kremlin's museums, you will find souvenir-stands selling books, albums, guidebooks, sets of pictures, videocassettes, CDs, and a vast variety of Kremlin-related memorabilia.

It is easy to get to the Kremlin's museums by subway: stops «Alexandrovskiy Sad», «Borovitskaya», «Biblioteka Imeni Lenina», «Arbatskaya» (exit towards the Alexandrov Gardens). Starting from subway stops «Teatralnaya», «Okhotniy Ryad», «Ploshchad Revolyutsii», it is a 5 to 10-minute walk. Mind you, if you are riding a car, you will have a hard time trying to find a parking slot near the Kremlin.

For further information, please call: (095) 202–3776 (answering machine) or (095) 203–0349 (excursions)

You can have most recent information related to the current cultural events held in the Kremlin's museums at www.kremlin.museum.ru.

MOSCOW KREMLIN

A GUIDE

THE STATE HISTORICAL AND CULTURAL
MUSEUM-RESERVE «THE MOSCOW KREMLIN»
MOSCOW 2002 ART-COURIER

Managing editor
Lydia Zakharova

Compiled by
Olga Dmitriyeva

Research Consultant
Asya Romanenko

Translator
Oleg Alyakrinsky

Design
Alexander Konoplev

Page-making, illustrations
Kirill Ivanov

Original photographs
Victor Seryogin

Reprinted photographs
(on pp. 2, 30–32, 90–91)
Nikolai Rakhmanov

ISBN 5-93842-017-2

CONTENTS

THE FORTRESS ON THE BOROVITSKIY HILL: A BRIEF HISTORY

The Kremlin – is the cradle of Moscow, the ancient city that was destined to consolidate disparate principalities and to become the capital of the centralized state of Russian. The history of the Moscow Kremlin, the nation's political, spiritual and cultural center, has been embodied in its monumental walls and towers, golden-domed cathedrals and churches, magnificent palaces. Especially majestic is the view on the Kremlin from the Kamenniy Bridge. In our time, this glorious vista is perhaps well known around the world. However, eight centuries ago, both the walls and the towers, and the buildings inside the Kremlin looked differently.

The Kremlin in the times of Ivan Kalita. Watercolor by A. Vasnetsov. 1920s.

From time immemorial, this place attracted men. Archeologists have discovered traces of the first settlements on the Borovitskiy Hill dating back to the late third and mid-second millennia B. C. The hill surrounded on both sides by water obstacles (the Moskva and the Neglinnaya Rivers), had a favorable location and enjoyed natural safety. Apparently, first settlers in this woody outback well appreciated the defensive potential of the Borovitskiy Hill. That is why powerful fortified walls were erected here.

Left: The Spasskaya Tower. November 1917.

The earliest mention of Moscow was dated back to the 12th century. The so-called Ipatiyevskaya Chronicle of the 15th century reported that in the year of 1147 Suzdal Prince Yuri Dolgorukiy invited Novgorod-Severskiy Prince Svyatoslav Olgovich to «Moscowe» to share a dinner. In all likelihood, by then Moscow was a rather large settlement where to host a distinguished guest along with his guard. According to the Tverskaya Chronicle of the 15th century, the son of Yuri Dolgorukiy, Andrei Bogolyubskiy, in 1156 built, upon his father's instruction, a wooden fortress on the Borovitskiy Hill, detinets, surrounded by a stockade and a wooden fence to protect its residents from alien attacks.

Daniil Alexandrovich, the son of the renowned Russian warlord, Prince Alexander Nevskiy, was Moscow's first Prince who, while adorning the Kremlin, erected a number of white-stone cathedrals – perhaps, instead of earlier wooden ones. In 1339–40, in the time of Prince Ivan Danilovich nicknamed «Kalita» (i. e. «money-bag»), an impressive oak citadel

Metropolitan Peter. Icon «Metropolitan with His Life Story» (Detail). 15th century.

was constructed on the Borovitskiy Hill whose walls were 2 to 6 meters thick and no less than 7 meters high. By the way, the very word «Kremlin» as related to the defensive structures above the Moskva River was first used in the Voskresenskaya Chronicle in an entry about the 1331 fire. Historians assume that the word could have been derived from the Old Russian «kremnik» meaning a fortress made of pinewood. However, according to a different point of view, the word «kremlin» may be traced back to the word «krom» or «kroma» meaning «edge», «frontier», as Moscow was a frontier outpost on the edge of the Vladimir Principality.

At that time, Moscow was a major political and commercial center. After Metropolitan Peter, the head of the Russian Orthodox Church, moved to Moscow from Vladimir in 1325, the city came to be the center of Old Russia's religious life, as well. From 1329 to 1333, a number of

The white-stone Kremlin. Watercolor by A. Vasnetsov. 1920s.

stone churches were built in Moscow, including the Archangel's Church founded in the name of Archangel Michael on the site where the old church of the same name once stood. In it, Ivan Kalita and other Moscow princes were buried.

Oak walls and towers had stood for only three decades and were destroyed by a terrible fire in the summer of 1365. Such was the sad demise of Moscow's first fortress on the Moskva River...

The defensive tasks required that Moscow would have a stronger and more reliable citadel. Ivan Kalita's 16-year-old grandson Dmitry who was then the ruling Prince of Moscow decided to build a stonewall fortress that would allow the citizens to defend the city from any adversary. In the second half of the 14th century, the Golden Horde in the East,

Ivan Kalita and Protsiy. Icon «Metropolitan with His Life Story» (Margin).

Lithuania in the Northwest and the hostile Russian principalities threatened the young Moscow Principality.

In the spring of 1367, the first stone was laid in the foundation of the new walls made of white stone. The white-stone Kremlin was a fast growing project – it was completed in just

A map of the white-stone Kremlin's defensive structures. 14th century. Reconstruction by V. Feodorov.

Contemporary redbrick walls are marked by a black line, white-stone walls, by a red line (dotted line shows sections where white-stone and red-brick walls coincide, continuous line shows sections where white-stone and redbrick walls do not coincide).
1. The Assumption Cathedral
2. The Church of John the Ladder-builder
3. The Church of Savior's on the Bor
4. The Annunciation Cathedral
5. The Archangel's Cathedral
6. The Cathedral of the Archangel's Wonder
7. The Church of Paraskeva of Friday
8. The Church of John the Precursor

Nicholas I's procession near the Chudov Monastery. P. Gerasimov. Mid-19th century.

Dmitry Donskoi. The Kremlin's Faceted Chamber. Late 19th century.

one year. Since that time, Moscow was to be called «the white-stoned city». We do not know the names of the builders. According to some evidence, the construction works on concrete sites were supervised by boyars (Russian noblemen) Ivan Sobaka, Feodor Sviblo, brothers Feodor and Frol Beklemishchevs. Later, the new towers of the white-stone fortress were called after their names and the names of their neighboring estates – Sobakina Tower (now Uglovaya Arsenalnaya) Sviblova Tower (now Vodovzvodnaya), Beklemishchevskaya.

The construction of the white-stone Kremlin was an important event in the history of the northeastern Old Russia as it marked the rise of Moscow Princes. Furthermore, the newly built fortress was tested for durability, in a war with Lithuanian prince Olgerd who besieged Moscow in 1368. The Lithuanian troops stood for three nights and days at Moscow's white-stone walls. Yet, the stronghold proved to be quite secure.

In August of 1380, while the rock-solid fortress was looming large behind their back, Russian troops led by

Prince Dmitry were encouraged to launch a decisive operation against the Tartar-Mongol invaders. Starting from the Kremlin's walls southward, to the mouth of the Don River, they faced Mamay's troops and defeated them in the now famous Battle on the Kulikovo Field. Prince Dmitry was nicknamed Donskoi (in 1989, he was sanctified by the Russian Orthodox Church in the memory of his glorious victory).

During a hundred years after the Kulikovo Battle, the white-stone fortress atop the Borovitskiy Hill dragged, like a magnet, the neighboring principalities and finally came to be the veritable unifying center of the Old Russia that towards the end of the 15th century had liberated itself from the Mongol-Tartar yoke. It might seem then that the white-stone walls could stand for centuries. However, the second fortress did not last long...

It was Prince Ivan III Vassiliyevich, who was nicknamed the Great and assumed the title of the Ruler of All Russia, who built the present-day red-brick walls and towers of the Moscow Kremlin. A massive construction project, initiated upon his order in 1485 and lasted for ten years, was not a mere renovation of Dmitry Donskoi's then battered fort even though the builders of the new Kremlin had reproduced the unique layout of the Old Russian fortress-detinets, while its territory retained its irregular triangular outline.

The southern border was the young nation's Achilles' heel; therefore, Moscow expected potential enemies to come from the southern approaches to the capital. That is why the builders started erecting a new fortress on the Moskva River on the south side. In 1485, Italian engineer Antonio Gilardi from Vicenza built the strong Tainitskaya Tower on the site where the Cheshkov Gate of the white-stone Kremlin earlier stood. In 1487, Italian engineer Marco Fryazin built the Beklemishchevskaya corner-tower; one year later, the Sviblova (or Vodovzvodnaya) corner-tower appeared on the opposite side of the wall.

Bringing the Big Council Bell of Novgorod to Moscow in 1478.

Great Prince Ivan III. Miniature from «The Czar's Title-book». 1672.

The Tainitskaya Tower. View from the Sophiyskaya Embankment.

By the early 1490, the southern side was completed: four more towers were erected (Blagoveshchenskaya, 1st and 2nd Bezymyannaya and Petrovskaya) and new walls were built at the foot of the Borovitskiy Hill.

The Petrovskaya Tower (cross-section plan).

The Tainitskaya Tower. View from the Kremlin.

In the 1490s, the Kremlin project was supervised by Pietro Antonio Solari (alias Peter Fryazin) from Milan, Italy, whose assistants were other Italians: Antonio Gilardi (alias Anton Fryazin) and Aloisio de Carcano (alias Aleviz Fryazin). At that time, the Kremlin had finally become the majestic and indestructible fortress as we can see it today.

The well in the Uglovaya Arsenalniya Tower.

The construction work was conducted taking into account the contemporary achievements of the practical science of fortification that in the 15th – early 16th century bloomed thanks to the invention and rapid improvement of offensive and defensive artillery. The leading engineers and builders of the Moscow Kremlin were Italian-born. At that time, Italy was Europe's leader in the theory and practice of fortification projects.

Every tower was a separate fortress in itself (especially, the pass- and corner-towers, which were absolutely invulnerable) and it could withstand hostile attacks even if in case an adversary would have taken the neighboring walls and towers. It was possible to get into these towers' upper floors by ladders through narrow gaps in the arched ceilings. In danger, the Kremlin's defenders could move around inside the walls by secret underground passages and concentrate the forces in critical points of defense or retreat when unable to counter the hostile offensive. Also, the so-called «slukhs» were dug out: these were long underground galleries, which were used both as secret watching points to keep surveillance for adversary preparations and as sites from where to launch sudden attacks.

In the 15th century, the towers were crowned with wooden marquees with watch-turrets; some towers were provided with alarm bells. Over the main gate, miracle-working icons were fixed. Double-sloped wooden roofs that were both a defensive device and a shelter against bad weather covered the walls.

Some towers had special functions, besides defensive ones. For instance, the Tainitskaya Tower had a secret passage from the fortress towards the Moskva River. In the Beklemishchevskaya, the Svib-lova (Vodovzvodnaya) and the Sobakina (Uglovaya Arsenalnaya) corner-towers, secret wells were dug out to supply water to the city when besieged.

By 1495, the new walls and towers of the fortress had been completed. However, the Kremlin was to be further reinforced.

In 1508, Great Prince Vassiliy Ivanovich, Ivan III's son, ordered to dig a moat facing Red Square to link the Moskva and the Neglinnaya. The Alevizov Moat (named after the project's supervisor Aleviz Fryazin), 32 m wide and 12 m deep, was filled with water from special reservoirs on the Neglinnaya. Along its rims and along the Moskva River, extra brick walls were built. So, the Kremlin had turned into a sort of an island that was hard to reach on any side, as it was only possible to get into the fortress via drawbridges at the pass-towers. To ensure that the fortress would be fireproof and would provide good view in all directions, the lands beyond the Neglinnaya and the Moskva River were cleared of all wooden structures. On a large slope near the magnificent Borovitskiy Hill, the so-called Czar's Garden was created. It had been there until the end of the 17th century. This sanitary and technical project had

Czar Mikhail Feodorovich Romanov. Miniature from «The Czar's Title-book». 1672.

The Faceted Chamber.

The Archangel's Cathedral. View from Cathedral Square.

also an aesthetic meaning, too: the vistas of the Borovitskiy Hill once chaotically dotted by shabby outhouses were at last seen in all its majestic vastness.

Enclosed by a red-brick necklace of the walls and towers, the Kremlin's territory had eventually expanded to its present-day size – about 27.5 hectares; its walls are 2,235 m long. At that time, a new Great Prince's palace was built in the Kremlin, whose parade hall – the Faceted Chamber –

Czar Peter I. Unknown artist. Second half of the 18th century. Detail.

The Ivan the Great Bell-Tower complex and the Czar Bell. View from Ivanov Square.

has survived until today. Back then, the Kremlin's main cathedrals- the Assumption, the Annunciation, and the Archangels – were built, as well as the cyclopic Ivan the Great Bell-tower.

Over the past five centuries, the events and the people have left many an imprint on the face of Moscow's proud fortress. The most dramatic was the fate of its southern side. In 1547, Moscow was destroyed by yet another fire. The flames took to the Kremlin's walls, and caused an explosion of powder stored in the cellars of the Petrovskaya, the 1st and 2nd Bezymyannaya Towers. The destroyed walls and towers were then reconstructed, but in 1571, Crimean Khan Devlet-Girey came to Moscow and burned it down.

In early 17th century, under Czar Boris

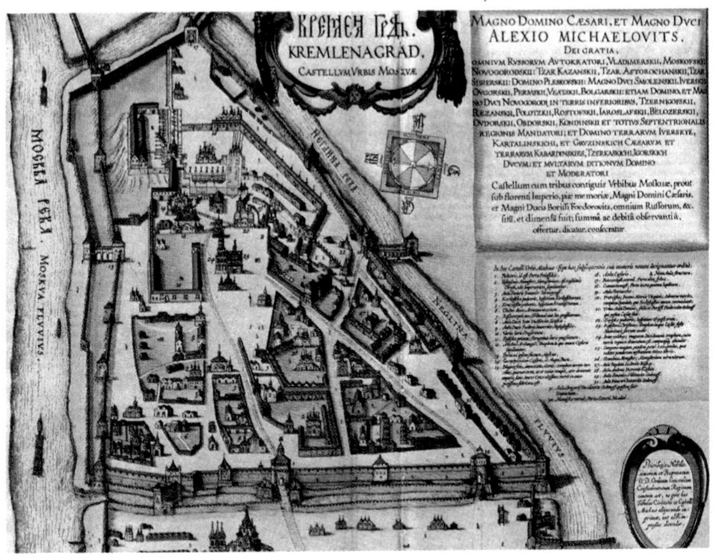

«Kremlinograd» – the Kremlin's map. Early 1600s.

Godunov and especially the first czars of the Romanov dynasty, many construction projects in the Kremlin's territory were underway. Instead of dilapidated wooden ones, new stone palaces were erected (including the Terem Palace, a major masterpiece of its time), as well as the new residence of the Russian Orthodox Church's leader, the Patriarch's Palace.

In 1670–80s, all the Kremlin's towers were overbuilt with stone marquees with beautiful tiled roofs. During the Northern War of 1707–08, Czar Peter the Great ordered to conduct fortification work in the Kremlin aimed at reinforcing its defensive potential. New bastions were made of earth. These stockades had stood for a hundred years and were removed only after the 1812 Patriotic War. The earth was then used to fill the moat along Red Square and to lay out the Alexandrov Gardens along the Kremlin's western wall (the project supervised by Ossip Bove was completed in 1817–1821).

In the late 18th century, upon the order of Empress Katherine II, the outstanding Russian architect Vassiliy Bazhenov embarked on building the Kremlin's new Imperial Palace. Following Bazhenov's project, the Tainitskaya, the 1st and 2nd Bezymyannaya and the Petrovskaya Towers were dismantled, along with the adjacent parts of the wall. However, the large-scale construction project soon was suspended, as the coffers lacked enough money due to the then ongoing Russo-Turkish War. The walls and the towers of the Kremlin's southern façade were completely restored, but they did not last long. In 1812, during Napoleon's invasion, the Sviblova (Vodovzvodnaya), the Tainitskaya, the Petrovskaya the 1st and 2nd Bezymyannaya Towers were blown up and seriously damaged by the fire. However, all the Kremlin's structures destroyed or damaged by Napoleon's troops were reconstructed in 1816–1835, under the supervision of architect Ossip Bove.

The last major construction project carried out in the Kremlin's territory in the 19th century was the Kremlin's Large Palace, built under the supervision of architect Kon-

The Kremlin. View from the Moskva River. Photograph. Early 20th century.

Red Square.

stantin Ton. According to the architect's design, this grandiose ensemble must have comprised both the old and the new buildings, both secular and religious. The monumental edifice of the Large Palace, the key component of the new architectural complex, was erected in 1836–47 where the old residence of Moscow's Great Prince (and later, Czar) once stood. Inside the inner year, they preserved the ancient Terem Palace together with home churches of Russian czars.

Until the early 18th century, Moscow had remained the Russian capital city, whereas the Kremlin, the official home of secular and religious leaders of the nation. After Peter the Great transferred the capital up to St. Petersburg, the city he built on the Neva River, and abolished the Patriarchate, the Kremlin lost its stately status. However, some state events of special importance, like coronation ceremonies, were still held in the Moscow Kremlin.

Vladimir Lenin in his Kremlin study. October 1918.

In 1918, the newly established Bolshevik government moved from the war-torn St. Petersburg (then Petrograd) to Moscow and landed in the Kremlin's Senate building. Moscow was re-established as the Russian capital, and the Kremlin regained its status of the nation's political center and the official home of the new regime. Early leaders of the Soviet Union lived and worked in the Kremlin's old buildings. In the last decades of the Soviet regime, most important state events were held in the Kremlin, where in the early 1960s a new official building was erected, the Kremlin's Palace of Congresses (now, the Kremlin's State Palace).

Since 1991, the Kremlin has been the official residence of the President of the Russian Federation. The cathedrals of the Moscow Kremlin have recently resumed their important role in the life of the Russian Orthodox Church now that holiday liturgies and special church services are conducted in them.

Unfortunately, the ancient Kremlin suffered irrevocable losses in the 20th century: the old Ascension Nunnery and Chudov Monastery, along with a number of outstanding cathedrals, were demolished. In the early 1930s, the Kremlin's territory was closed for the general public. Only in June of 1955, the Kremlin once again opened its gates to let in visitors.

In December of 1990, by the UNESCO's decision, the architectural ensembles of the Moscow Kremlin and Red Square were included in the World Heritage list.

The Christmas Tree in Cathedral Square. 2002.

THE TOWERS OF THE KREMLIN

The Kremlin's charming appeal is unlimited. You can come here in any season of the year: in winter when the sparkling snow emphasizes the whiteness of its cathedrals; in spring when the Kremlin is as if covered by a filigree green canopy; in summer when its gardens are in full bloom... For over five centuries, the Kremlin has been protected by the merloned redbrick walls and 20 mighty towers.

The Kremlin walls' merlon.

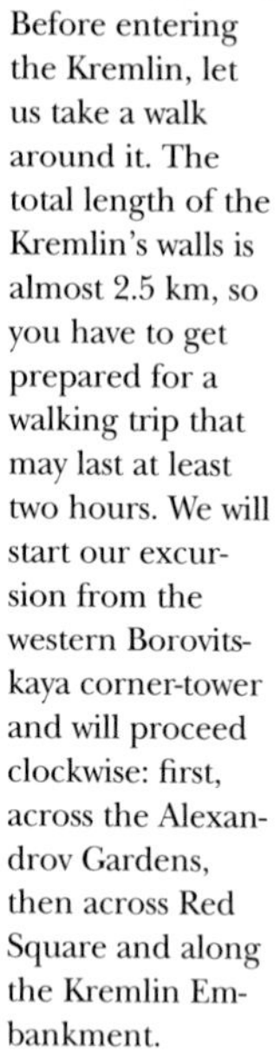

Before entering the Kremlin, let us take a walk around it. The total length of the Kremlin's walls is almost 2.5 km, so you have to get prepared for a walking trip that may last at least two hours. We will start our excursion from the western Borovitskaya corner-tower and will proceed clockwise: first, across the Alexandrov Gardens, then across Red Square and along the Kremlin Embankment.

The Borovitskaya Tower, like, was named after the grove (Russian «bor») that in the days of old covered the Borovitskiy Hill's southeastern slope. According to another theory, the name of the hill was derived from Borovsk, a major commercial center of that time; the builders who were engaged in 1366–1367 in the «white-stone Kremlin» construction project on this spot came from Borovsk. The tower was built in 1490 by Italian architect Pietro Antonio Solari. In the 16–17th century, the gate was used as an entrance to the Kremlin's services area. In 1658, the tower was renamed Predtechenskaya (alias the Baptist's), after the Church of John the Baptist Under the Bor that stood nearby in the Kremlin's territory. However, the new name did not last long, and in the 19th century it was given again its previous name. From the mid-17th century on, the tower was topped with a double-headed eagle, which in 1935 was substituted by a steel star with a hammer and a sickle in its center. Two years later, the steel star gave way to an illumined ruby one. The tower's height without the star is 50.7 m; with the star – 54.05 m.

The Borovitskaya Tower.

The neighboring Oruzheinaya (Armory) Tower was built in 1493–1495. It was first called

The Moscow Kremlin's southern wall.

Konyushennaya (the Stables'), after the nearby Stables Court. The present-day name was given to it in 1851, after the Oruzheinaya (Armo-

The Oruzheinaya Tower.

ry) Chamber was built in its vicinity. In early 17th century, it was a pass-tower, and its passage led to the Kremlin's Stables Court. In 1676– 1686, a marquee top was added as an extra adornment. The Tower's entrance is on the inside. Its height is 38.9 m. Its perimeter at the base is 35 m long. Its walls are 1.7 to 2.4 m thick.

Moving on along the alleys of the Alexandrov Gardens, you reach the Komendantskaya Tower. It was erected in 1493–1495. Originally, it was called Kolymazhnaya (Carriages'), because a Carriages Court, a sort of a royal carriage pool, was located close to it in the Kremlin's territory. In the 19th century, the tower was given its present-day name, after the Kremlin's commandant settled in the nearby Fun Palace. The Tower consists of five levels and a watch-turret. Its height as seen from the Alexandrov Gardens is 41.25 m.

The next one, the majestic Troitskaya (Trinity) Tower is the Kremlin's highest pass-tower. Once, its gate was used as the main passage leading to the Patriarch's Palace and the Czarina

The Komendantskaya Tower.

and Czarevnas' quarters. Its perimeter at the base is 85.7 m long. The walls are 5.7 to 6.4 m thick. The Tower was built by Aleviz Fryazin in 1495–1499 and it has had many names: it was first called Bogoyavlenskaya (Epiphany's), after the main church of the Troitskiy monastery; then it was called Rizpolozhenskaya (Our Lady's Sacred Robe), after the nearby Church of Our Lady's Holy Robe; then Znamenskaya (Holy Sign), after the icon of Our Lady's Holy Sign that was hung above its gate, and Karetnaya (Carriage's).

The Troitskaya Tower.

The Troitskaya Tower's steel star. 1935.

Lastly, in 1658, it was named Troitskaya, after the Troitskiy Monastery that was located nearby. In the 17th century, the tower was topped with a double-headed eagle. In 1935, the czarist eagle was substituted by the Soviet steel star bearing the hammer-and-sickle emblem. Two years later, the steel star was replaced by an illuminated ruby one. Its

The Kutafiya Tower.

height without the star (on the Kremlin's side) is 65.65 m; its height together with the star is 69.3 m. Its walls are 5.7 to 6.4 m thick.

In 1516, Aleviz Fryazin built a stone bridge over the Neglinnaya connecting the tower's strelnitsa and a new watchtower – the Kutafiya Tower. It protected the approaches to the Troitskaya Tower and the bridge. The Kutafiya Tower is roofless and is all filled with air. Its name was derived from the Old Russian word «kut» – «shelter», «corner», and «peninsula». Originally, it was 18 m high and was surrounded by a moat and the river. It had a gate 6 m above the ground and a sloping drawbridge that firmly shut the gateway. In 1685, it was decorated with a filigree white-stone crown with carved elements. In 1868, during a renovation, a passageway was cut out in the western wall to let the city traffic onto the Troitskiy Bridge, while the old side-gate was filled with brickwork. On the southern side, a sentry box was installed. In 1976–77, the Kutafiya Tower was renovated: the sentry box was dismantled, the side archways were restored, and the whole structure was dyed again in two colors. Its present-day height is 13.5 m. Its walls are ca. 2 m thick.

Before our story about the Kremlin's towers continues, let us draw your attention to the Alexandrov Gardens' highlights. Back in the times of Ivan the Terrible, the Aptekarskiy Gardens were set up on the Neglinnaya's right bank, between the Borovitskaya and Troitskaya Towers. But already in early 19th century, this old Moscow's downtown was all swamps and ravines turned into the city's garbage pit.

In 1817–23, in commemoration of Russia's glorious victory over Napoleon, this desolate land was miraculously recreated, under a huge parking project supervised by Ossip Bove, into the Kremlin Gardens that in 1856 was renamed Alexandrov, after Emperor Alexander I. The vast territory of the new Gardens stretched from the Borovitskaya Tower to the Uglovaya Arsenalniya Tower was divided into three parts: the Upper, the Middle and the Lower Gardens. In 1821, a decorative grotto with a small hill

The grotto in the Alexandrov Gardens.

and a brass-band floor decorated with white-stone elements was built at the tower's base, according to architect Ossip Bove's design. On June 10, 1913, the Obelisk in commemoration of the tercentennial of the Romanov dynasty was opened in the Upper Gardens. In 1918, upon Lenin's instruction, the Obelisk was modernized in both form and essence. The coats of arms and the czars' names were removed. The new Soviet symbol – hammer and sickle – and the initials of the new state «RSFSR» (Russian Soviet Federative Socialist Republic) were carved on the pedestal and the Obelisk was covered by the engraved names of Socialist thinkers and political activists.

In December 1966, when the Muscovites celebrated the 25th anniversary of the Nazi's defeat at Moscow, the Unknown Soldier Memorial was set up near the Uglovaya Arsenalnaya Tower. On the right of the tomb, 12 dark-red porphyry slabs were set up with capsules filled with soil brought from Russian war-hero cities: Leningrad, Kiev, Minsk, Stalingrad, Sebastopol, Odessa, Kerch, Novorossiysk, Tula, Murmansk, Smolensk and the Brest Fortress. The Unknown Soldier Memorial is guarded day and night by sentries from the Kremlin regiment. Changing of the guards occurs every hour (every half-hour in wintertime).

Now back to our walking tour. The Sredniya Arsenalnaya (Middle Arsenal) Tower was built in 1493–95 to replace the old white-stone Kremlin's corner tower. Before the 18th century, it was called the Granyonnaya (Faceted) Tower, and it was given its present-day name after the Arsenal was built in the Kremlin's territory. The tower's height is 38.9 m. Its walls are 2.5 to 5 m thick.

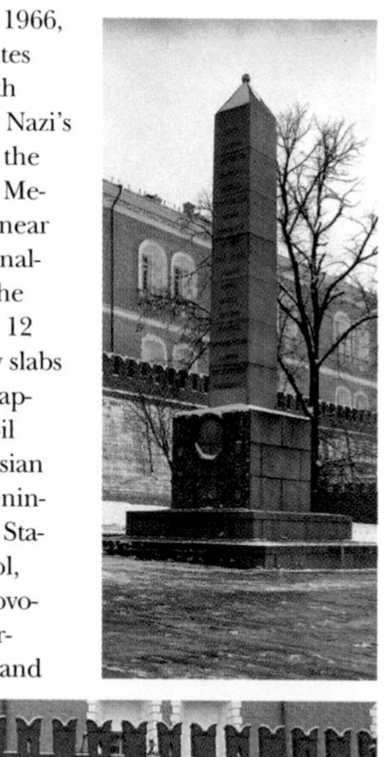

The Obelisk in the Alexandrov Gardens.

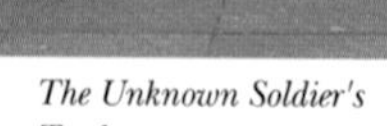

The Unknown Soldier's Tomb.

Its neighbor, the Uglovaya Arsenalnaya (Arsenal Corner) Tower, is a little older. It was erected in 1492 by Pietro Antonio Solari. Until the 18th century, the Tower bore a different name – Sobakina – after the adjacent boyars Sobakins' estate. This strong and massive tower (its walls are 6 m thick, its height on the Alexandrov Gardens' side is 60.2 m) protected the ferry across the Neglinnaya to the marketplace in Red Square and housed a water source. The springwater well is still there in the tower's deep cellar. Curiously, the well water did not bring harm to either the Tower' brickwork or the archives that it housed

The Sredniya Arsenalnaya Tower.

in the late 19th century. Originally, the Tower had seven rows of loopholes and a secret exit to the Neglinnaya River; in 1670–86, the rows of loopholes were all filled. After the 1946–57 renovation, the Tower regained its look of the mid-17th century.

The Alexandrov Gardens ends near the

The Uglovaya Arsenalnaya Tower.

Uglovaya Arsenalniya Tower. Leaving the Alexandrov Gardens through its filigree wrought iron gate and turning to the right, you will make your way to Red Square. On your left, you will see the History Museum, a majestic dark redbrick edifice in the pseudo-Russian style (architect W. Sherwood). The Museum was opened in 1883.

In 1994–96, the Voskresenskiye Gate was reconstructed on the

The Voskresenskiy Gate and the Iverskaya Chapel.

other side of the History Museum. The stone Voskresenskiye (Resurrection) Gate to Red Square was built in 1680 and dismantled in the early 1930s. On coronation days and special holidays, Russian Czars always entered the Kremlin via the Voskresenskiye Gate from Tverskaya Street. Adjacent to the Gate, the small Chapel of Iverskaya Mother of God was erected in the name of the 12th century miracle-working namesake icon that Muscovites revered as the city's treasure. The chapel was destroyed along with the Voskresenskiye Gate in the early 1930s and it was reconstructed together with the latter.

Along the Kremlin's northeastern wall, a vast cobbled square stretches out, the main square of not only Moscow but also all Russia. Here, popular mass festivities are held on national holidays, and even open-air public concerts are organized.

In ancient times, this square – a far too smaller back then – housed the city's marketplace. From 1625 on, a site in between the Spasskaya Tower, the Vassiliy the Blessed Cathedral and the Lob-

The Alexandrov Gardens' fence. Fragment.

noye Spot was called Krasnaya (Red), which in Old Russian meant «beautiful». Towards the end of the 17th century, the name «Red Square» was given over to the whole large plot of vacant land in front of the Kremlin. In the 1680s, the square was covered with wooden planks, and in 1804, it was cobble-stoned for the first time. In the 20th century, Red Square came to be a stage for official events held in Moscow.

The first on the northeastern wall is

the Nikolskaya Tower. It was given its name after the icon of St. Nicholas the Miracle-Worker that once hung over the gate of the Tower's side-

The Nikolskaya Tower.

strelnitsa facing Red Square. Pietro Antonio Solari built the Tower in 1491. In those times, the Tower had a clock installed in it. A drawbridge at the side-strelnitsa let visitors pass over the moat on Red Square and enter the Kremlin. In the early 18th century, the Tower was rebuilt by the famous architect Bartholomeo Rastrelli. Its top was damaged in an 1812 explosion, and the Tower was restored in 1816 according to Ossip Bove's design. Until 1935, the double-headed eagle crowned the Nikolskaya Tower. Then, a star made of stainless steel and coated with gilt red copper replaced it. The «Hammer and Sickle» emblem inlaid with precious stones was fixed on the star's both sides. In 1937, a new ruby star illuminated from within was installed instead of the steel one. Its height (without the star) is 67.1 m; its height together with the star is 70.4 m. Its walls are 4.5 m thick.

Almost exactly in the middle of this portion of the Kremlin's wall, the Senatskaya Tower stands. It was built in 1491 by Pietro Antonio Solari and its entrance is located on the Kremlin's inside. Until the late 18th century, it had remained nameless and only in 1787, after the Senate building was erected in the Kremlin, the Tower was given its present-day appellation. Its height is 34.3 m. The walls are 3.3 m thick.

The royal eagle is being dismantled from the Kremlin's tower (above) and replaced by a star (below). 1935.

Right in front of the Senatskaya Tower you can see a squat and flat-topped pyramidal edifice of marble. This is Lenin's Mausoleum built in 1930 (architect A. Shchusev). It houses the mummified body of Vladimir Lenin, the leader of the 1917 Bolshevik revolution. In 1953, after the then Soviet leader Josef Stalin died in early March, his mummified body was put in the Mausoleum, as well; but in 1961, Stalin's body was removed and buried at the Kremlin's wall, in

The Senatskaya Tower.

the revolutionary necropolis. The tradition to bury at the Kremlin's wall the bodies of leaders of the international communist and workers' movement, outstanding Soviet statesmen and public figures, men of arts and major war heroes, pilots and cosmonauts was initiated in the mid-1920s. As of today, over 300 men and women rest in piece at the Kremlin's wall.

Opposite the Senatskaya Tower, across Red Square, you can see a long three-story structure erected in pseudo-Russian style. It is the GUM department store, formerly known the Upper Shopping Rows that were built in 1894 according to the design of architect A. Pomerantsev.

While on Red Square you will hear the melodious ringing of the chimes on the Spasskaya Tower. The Kremlin's most famous tower was built in 1491 by Pietro Antonio Solari on the site of the ancient white-stone Kremlin's Frolovskaya strelnitsa. Up to the 17th century, this pass-tower was called Frolovskaya, as it stood near the Frol and Laur Church inside the Kremlin. The tower protected the Kremlin's northeastern approaches that lacked natural obstacles. Its double walls were made of oversized bricks. An in-wall staircase connected all the five levels of the Tower. A wooden draw-

The Revolution necropolis near the Kremlin wall. Photograph. 1920s.

Lenin's Mausoleum on Red Square.

bridge was built over the moat at the Tower's gate. In 1624–25, the Spasskaya Tower was the Kremlin's first one to be overbuilt: a high octahedron on top of a stepped quadrihedron and crowned with a high eight-faceted marquee was added to the original building.

In 1658, according to the Czar's decree, the tower of the Kremlin's main gate was renamed Spasskaya, after the gate-icons of the Savior Almighty of Smolensk (on Red Square's side) and Veronica (on the Kremlin's side). From then on, the slender gorgeous tower, with lavish white-stone carved décor, was recognized as the Kremlin's main tower. Through the Spasskiye Gate, the Czars' ceremonial exits proceeded on holidays and the military units marched on parade, as well as foreign ambassadors entered the Kremlin to meet the Russian monarchs. It was strictly forbidden to pass through the Gate on horseback or with a headwear on.

The Tower's foremost adornment was the clock with chimes made and installed in 1625 by a British clockmaker Christopher Galloway. A Russian caster Kirill Samoilov cast 13 bells – one big one for striking hours and twelve smaller ones for striking quarter-hours. The clock had a revolving dial, whose face was dyed in azure; the stars and the Moon were over-painted in gold and silver, and the gold-painted Sun was fixed above, and its long beam pointed to the hours on the dial.

The Spasskaya Tower.

In 1706–09, upon Czar Peter the Great's instruction, a new clock and chimes were installed in the tower. Both were made in Amsterdam and delivered by sea to Russia's port of Archangelsk in thirty big boxes. The Brothers Butenop Company installed the present-day clock and chimes in 1851–52. clockwork

The bells of the Spasskaya Tower's chimes.

The famous Kremlin's clock.

occupies three stories and consists of three blocks: main mechanism, hour-striking mechanism and quarter-hour-striking mechanism. The clock has four dials located on every side of the tower; each dial is 6.12 m in diameter; the dial numbers are 72 cm high; the hour hand is 2.97 m long and the minute hand is 3.28 m long. Hours are marked in gilded Roman numbers, minutes are marked in small squares. A 32-kg pendulum maintains the accuracy of the clock's mechanism.

The Pokrovskiy Cathedral.

The Minin and Pozharskiy Monument.

A Kremlin star.

The total weight of the clockwork is ca. 25 tons.

When in 1935, the Soviet leaders decided to remove from the Spasskaya, Nikolskaya, Borovitskaya and Troitskaya Towers the double-headed eagles and replace them with five-pointed stars; the Spasskaya Tower was the first to have the facelift. Illuminated by spotlights from below, the big steel star had topped the Kremlin's major tower for two years. Eventually a smaller ruby star re-

The Lobnoye Spot.

placed it. The star's surface was evenly and brightly illuminated from the inside by uniquely powerful lamps of 3,700 to 5,000 W that were shining day and night. The Tower's height is 67.3 m without the star and 71 m together with the star. Its walls are 3.6 m thick.

Close to the Spasskaya Tower, on Red Square's southern side, you can see the majestic and sophisticatedly beautiful Pokrovskiy Cathedral on the Moat (alias, the Basil the Blessed's Cathedral). It was erected on Czar Ivan the Terrible's order in 1555–1561 to commemorate the taking of Kazan and the conquest of the Astrakhan Khanate. The Cathedral incorporates 11 churches.

The eight lovely single-domed churches of stone stand symmetrically around the ninth, topped with a high marquee. This central component of the ensemble was dedicated to the Day of Our Lady's Holy Robe (in Russian: «Pokrov day»), the day Kazan was conquered. In 1588, the tenth church was erected on a gallery, over the tomb of Moscow's famed blessed man Vassiliy (Basil). The cathedral's alternative name – Basil the Blessed's – is associated with this tenth dome. Lastly, in 1672, the eleventh church was added: it was built over the tomb of Moscow's another blessed man Ivan the Blessed who was buried in the cathedral in 1589.

In 1818, in front of the Pokrovskiy Cathedral, the Monument to citizen Kuzma Minin and prince Dmitry Pozharskiy was put up (sculptor I. Martos). The two men are Russia's popular heroes who in 1612 led the revolt against the Polish invaders. A century later, the Monument was moved closer to the Pokrovskiy Cathedral.

A round dais on Red Square in front of the Spasskaya Tower – the Lobnoye Spot – has been known since in 1547. Legend has it that the most dangerous state criminals were decapitated on the Lobnoye Spot. However, these legends are mere fiction. From this public podium, the Kremlin's heralds recited the Czar's decrees. In the «Troubled Times», the Lobnoye Spot was used as a public pulpit: standing here in 1612, prince Dmitry Pozharskiy declared Moscow liberated from the Polish invaders. Up to 1597, the Lobnoye Spot was a wooden platform; afterwards, it was rebuilt in stone.

Going from the Lobnoye Spot back to the Spasskaya Tower and continuing your walk along the Kremlin's wall, you will see the rather small Czarskaya Tower that was put onto the wall in 1680. The tower's name reflects the old legend about a four-faceted wooden turret with Czar Ivan the Terrible's throne inside. From here, the legend says, the cruel Czar could keep close watch on what was going on in the Kremlin and on Red Square. An elegant eight-faceted marquee standing on four pitcher-shaped pillars and topped with gilded weathervane, reminds of Old Russian terem-buildings. In the Tower's marquee, the alarm bells of the Kremlin's fire brigade were once fixed. Over the centuries, the Tower's original look has been preserved. Its height (with a weathervane) is 16.7 m.

The next is the Nabatnaya (Alarm-Bell's) Tower erected in 1495. It was given its present-day name in 1658, when the major alarm bell of the Kremlin's fire brigade was stationed inside. During the 1771 plague, thousands of panic-stricken people could not find any other way to save themselves from the terrible disease rather than coming to the Kremlin's wonder-working icon of Our Lady with their prayers. When the authorities tried to forbid mass gatherings the so-called «Plague Riot» broke

The Czarskaya Tower.

The Nabatnaya Tower.

out. Its instigators struck the Nabatnaya Tower's bell calling the alerted people to the Kremlin. After the riot was suppressed, Czarina Katherine II ordered to «punish» the bell: she ordered to tear the «trouble-making» bell's tongue out. In the early 19th century, when the tower was under renova-

The Konstantino-Yeleninskaya Tower.

tion, the muted bell was removed and taken to the Kremlin's Arsenal. In 1851, it was transferred to the Armory Chamber. The Tower's height is 38 m. Its walls are 2.5 m thick.

The sturdy Konstantino-Yeleninskaya Tower was built in 1490 by Pietro Antonio Solari instead of the white-stone Kremlin's Timofeyevskiye Gate. At the time, it protected the adjacent borough and the approaches from the nearest Moskva River pier and the streets. A mighty side-strelnitsa was connected by a drawbridge with the tower's body. In 1658, the tower was given a new name, after the Sts. Constantine and Helen's Church that stood nearby. In the 17th century, the side-strelnitsa was refashioned into a prison. From then on, the tower housed the Robbers Department and was teasingly nicknamed the Torturing Chamber. It height is 36.8 m. Its walls are 3.3 m thick.

The Beklemishchevskaya Tower.

One of the Kremlin's oldest towers – the Beklemishchevskaya – stands at the corner of the Vassiliyevskiy Hill and the Kremlin Embankment. It was given its name after the boyar Nikita Beklemishchev's estate that was located near here, in the Kremlin's territory. Built in 1487–88 by Italian architect Marco Fryazin, instead of the ancient Kremlin's corner-tower, this round structure played a very important strategic role, as it protected the main ferry across the Moskva River. The tower's height is 46.2 m. Its walls are 2.3 m thick.

Walking up the Kremlin Embankment, you will find yourself at the Kremlin's southern wall. This is the last leg of our long stroll around the ancient fortress. Here you can see one by one seven towers standing rather close to each other and linked by the high merloned wall. The three of them had been erected for purely defensive reasons and remained nameless for quite a long time.

The Petrovskaya Tower.

The 2nd Bezymyannaya Tower.

Originally, the Petrovskaya (Peter's) Tower was called the 3rd Bezymyannaya; later it was renamed Ugreshskaya, after the adjacent Ugreshskiy monastery in the Kremlin's territory. In the 18th century, it was given its present-day name Petrovskaya after the Metropolitan of Moscow Peter's Church that was relocated inside the tower after the monastery was abolished in 1771. The Tower was built in 1480s. In peacetime, the Kremlin's gardeners used it. Its height is 27.15 m. The walls are 2 to 2.3 m thick.

The Petrovskaya Tower's immediate

neighbor was less lucky, as it was destined to remain nameless.

The 2nd Bezymyannaya (Nameless) Tower was built in 1487–88 and originally was a pass-tower with a gate. Its height is 30.2 m. Its walls are 1.8 to 2.1 m thick.

The 1st Bezymyannaya (Nameless) Tower was built in the 1480s. It used to be a powder storage and during the 1547 fire, it was seriously damaged by an explosion of the powder kept inside. The tower's height is 34.15 m. Its walls are 2.3 to 2.7 m thick.

The Tainitskaya (Secret) Tower, the oldest of the Kremlin's towers, was built in 1485 by Anton Fryazin instead of the old Kremlin's Cheshkov Gate. The tower was given its name after an underground passage that led towards the Moskva River. Its height is 38.4 m; the walls are 4.4 m thick.

The 1st Bezymyannaya Tower (left) and its cross-section plan (right).

The quadrangular Blagoveshchenskaya Tower was erected in 1485–88 and in the 1680s overbuilt with a stone marquee. It was given its name in the 18th century after the icon «Annunciation» installed on it. «Annunciation» installed on it.

In the 17th century, the Portomoyniye (literally, Pants-Washing) Gate was located near the tower. The Kremlin's laundresses would come out via the gate to a specialraft docked on the Moskva River and wash the clothes. In 1831, the gate was filled. The tower's height is 30.7 m without a weathervane, and 32.45 m together with a weathervane. Its walls are 1.3 to 2.3 m thick. shallow waters near the Neglinnaya River's mouth. Originally, there was a well inside its cellar, and an underground passage led to construction site, on the Kremlin's side. In 1633, a water-pumping machine was installed inside to take water from the Moskva and

The Tainitskaya Tower (left) and the Blagoveshchenskaya Tower (right).

The Vodovzvodnaya Tower. View from the Kammeniy Bridge.

send it to a lead-coated reservoir fixed in the upper part of the tower. After that, the Tower was called the Vodovzvodnaya, i. e. Water-Supplying. In 1937, a ruby star replaced its weathervane. Its height without the star is 57.7 m, together with the star – 61.25. Its walls are 2.2 m thick.

Getting back to the Borovitskaya Tower, you have completed the walking tour around the ancient fortress. And now let us go inside the museum reserve and admire the beauty of the Kremlin's cathedrals.

The last Vodovzvodnaya (Water Supplying) Tower stands at the corner of the Kremlin Embankment and the Alexandrov Gardens. Built in 1488 by Anton Fryazin it protected the the river. Until the 17th century, it had been called the Sviblova Tower after boyar Sviblo who was in charge of its construction and who had his estate adjacent to the

INSIDE THE KREMLIN

If you enter the Kremlin via the Borovitskiye Gate you can see on your left a yellow two-story building – the Armory Chamber. Walk along it to the high filigree cast-iron fence – and just stop for a while. Seven centuries ago, here stood the wooden Church of John the Baptist's Nativity, Moscow's first house of God...

Public festivities in Cathedral Square in commemoration of Alexander II's coronation. Lithograph based on Teihel's drawing. 1856.

The history of the Kremlin's cathedrals can be recovered by the testimonies – sometimes indirect – of the ancient chronicles. This, in 1461, while describing the construction of the stone John the Baptist's Nativity near the Borovitskiye Gate, the chronicler reported that «in this place, once there was a wooden church, the first one in the grove». Perhaps, this «first church in the grove» was erected soon after the local residents adopted Christianity, and apparently, it was the first Orthodox church in ancient Moscow. The church had stood there almost four centuries, and in 1847, the dilapidated stone structure was dismantled.

Passing by the next complex – the Kremlin's Large Palace, you will find yourself on Cathedral Square. Here, on the Moscow Kremlin's central parade square, stand the main memorials of the ancient Russian church architecture, the Kremlin's cathedrals.

From time immemorial, Cathedral Square had been Old Russia's center of political and social life. Here, public services were conducted in the open, religious processions with cross carrying rituals occurred on major church holidays, and spectacular coronation ceremonies were held. In front of the Faceted Chamber's Red Porch, foreign ambassadors were officially greeted. In the days of mourning, burial processions crossed the Square towards the Archangel's Cathedral, the burial place of Moscow Great Princes and Czars, and towards the Assumption Cathedral, the necropolis of Moscow Metropolitans and Patriarchs.

THE ASSUMPTION CATHEDRAL

The Assumption Cathedral is the key highlight of Cathedral Square. Built of white stone and remarkably harmonious – even despite its laconic design – the Cathedral strikes an onlooker with its majestic tranquility and magnificence. Its majestic body is topped with five mighty golden domes.

Initially, it was not only Old Russia's main church but also the country's key public building. At the Assumption Cathedral, besides regular services, inaugurations of Metropolitans and Patriarchs occurred, as well as many important church rituals and state events were held. Assumption). Most important state documents were kept in the Cathedral's altar. Since 1498, new Great Princes were crowned for reigning in the Cathedral (Dmitry, the grandson of Ivan III, was the first), and after 1547, new czars were given the Russian crown here (Ivan the Terrible was the first). Also, most important royal marriage ceremonies were held here. In this Cathedral, heads of the Russian Orthodox Church were buried. In here, upon the instruction of Czar Peter the Great, his son, prince Alexei, abdicated from his right for the royal crown, and Duke of Schleswig-Holstein, who briefly reigned in Russia under the name of Peter III, converted to Orthodox Christianity. After St. Petersburg was made the capital city of the Russian Empire in 1712, the Assumption Cathedral did not lose its status as the nation's main church until the early 20th century. The key state ceremony, coronation of new Emperors and Empresses, was still held at the Assumption Cathedral.

According to archeological findings, in late 12th century here, on the highest point of the Borovitskiy Hill where the Assumption Cathedral stands today, a wooden church was built. In 1325, after Metropolitan Peter, the head of the Russian Orthodox Church, moved to Moscow, Prince Ivan Kalita ordered to erect a white-stone cathedral in the name of Our Lady's

The Assumption Cathedral's interior. Watercolor by A. Kolb. Second half of the 19th century.

Assumption, instead of the old wooden one. Towards the second half of the 15th century, the cathedral had almost dilapidated. Prince Ivan III in 1472 instructed builders Krivtsov and Myshkin to erect a new one instead. The construction in progress was a success. By the late spring of 1474, the walls had been completed. On May 20, the newly built structure crumbled down unexpectedly. The chronicle referred to one of the reasons as «great shaking», i. e. an earthquake. Bricklayers invited from Pskov, after having examined the ruins, refused to resume the construction works. Then, Ivan III decided to commission well-experienced foreign architects to build the Kremlin's main cathedral. A year later, in June of 1475, an Italian architect and engineer Aristotle Fiorovanti laid the foundation of the new cathedral that was consecrated in 1479.

The southern portal. Fragment.

The Cathedral has three entrances: southern, western, and northern ones. The southern door facing Cathedral Square, the ceremonial place, was devised as a parade entrance and was lavishly adorned. A wide staircase leads to the door and ends in a white-stone portal made of three gradually diminishing semicircular arches. Two angels are guarding the entrance. In the white-stone arches above them, there are figures of the saints, and still higher, an image of Our Lady with Christ on her arms.

Icon «Our Lady of Vladimir». Moscow. 1514.

In the course of centuries, the Assumption Cathedral's interior was changed many times; however, all those changes did not affect the original artistic design. In 1481, as the chronicle tells us, «icon-maker Dionysy and priest Timofey and Yarets and Konya» adorned it with a tri-tiered iconostasis and wall painting. Dionysy, an outstanding master of the Moscow school of painting of the late 15th-early 16th centuries, painted the

The Cathedral's interior.

Icon «Savior the Awesome Eye». 14th century.

Cathedral's main icon «Assumption» (the second one to the right of the king's gate in the iconostasis' lowest row). In the southern side of the iconostasis, you can see the true masterpieces «Judgment Day», «Apocalypse», «Of Thee Rejoices» and «Metropolitan Peter in His Hagiography» painted by Dionysy and the painters of his school.

The altar, in the Cathedral's eastern wing, was initially isolated from the rest of the building by a 3.5-meter high stone partition.

Icon «Of Thee Rejoices». Late 15th-early 16th century. Dionysy's workshop.

On it, from the northern wall to the southern one, at 2.5 meters above the floor, Dionysy painted portraits of 23 saints, monks and hermits. Originally, these portraits were incorporated into the iconostasis, but eventually the composition was hidden behind oak panels and the local tier's new icons. Only in the 1950s, some figures were revealed.

In all likelihood, Dionysy painted the compositions «John the Precursor's Nativity», «Our Lady's Appraisal»,

Icon «Saint George» (left) and its reverse side, «Our Lady Odigitry».

and «Worship of the Magi» in the Dmitrovsky and Pokhvalsky chapels attached to the altar on the southern side. To the north of the altar, in the Peter-and-Paul Chapel and in the altar's shrine, you can see the survived portions of the late 15th and 16th century wall paintings: «Apostle Peter Curing the Sick», «Seven Adolescents of Ephesus Sleeping», and «Forty Martyrs of Savasty». In the Cathedral, you can see the wall paintings of the Kremlin's mid-17th century artists.

The second and third rows of the wall paintings on the Assumption Cathedral's southern and northern walls are dedicated to Our Lady. The third upper tier depicts the so-called proto-Evangelical cycle: it is a story of Mary's life, of her parents Joachim and Anna. Below, is the Acathistus cycle – 18 illustrations to the Acathistus in honor of Virgin Mary, in which she is embodied as a guardian of the mankind, an intermediary between God and humans.

Of special interest are frescoes in the southern and northern walls' lower row. These are depictions of the seven Ecumenical Councils held in the 4–7th centuries, when higher church leaders set the basis of the Christian belief and outlined the relations between the religious and secular power. On the western wall, there is the traditional composition «The Judgment Day».

In the middle, you can see Christ as the King of Heaven and the Supreme Judge surrounded by apostles, saints and angels. Below him, on his right, there are the sinners facing avenge, whereas on his left, there are the righteous destined for «the eternal bliss». On the pillars, there are 135 images of the most revered Russian saints.

In 1653, the Cathedral was decorated with a new huge iconostasis. In contrast to the traditional Russian iconostasis, its deesis tier, apart from the Savior, Virgin Mary, John the Precursor and Archangels Michael and Gabriel, features the icons of the twelve apostles – just like in Greek cathedrals. The composition and arrangement of the local tier's icons were changed, too. The Assumption Cathedral's new iconostasis was made by a team of painters from Yaroslavl, Kostroma, Ostashkov. Among the painters were such famous icon-makers like Iosif Vladimirov and Konstantin Ananiyn.

The Cathedral houses an invaluable collection of works of art, with true international masterpieces among them. Such is, for instance, the Cathedral's most ancient double-sided icon «Saint Georgy» (dates back to the 12th century) with «Our Lady Odigitry» (mid-14th century) on its reverse side. It is displayed on the northern wall. «Savior the Awesome Eye» was painted in Moscow in the 1340s. It is located in the iconostasis' low row to the right, over the door to the deacon's room. An icon «The Savior in Shoulder-Length» (on the western wall) was painted almost in the

Icon «Savior in Shoulder-Length». 14th century.

Painting on the Cathedral's southern wall. Detail.

«Forty Martyrs of Sevasty». Fresco. 14th century. Detail.

same period. «Our Lady of Vladimir» is painted in the technique close to that of Andrei Rublev's. This is an early 15th century copy of the famous Byzantine icon of the 11–12th century. Another copy of «Our Lady of Vladimir», made in the early 16th century, and held in a silver holder, is in the local tier to the left of the king's gate.

Many icons displayed in the Assumption cathedral were painted in the 17th century. For example, in the northern side of the iconostasis, there is «The Trinity» painted by Tikhon Filatiyev on the old iconboard above the 14th-century layer that has been partly revealed (the head of an angel in the right corner).

Icon «The Trinity». Detail. 14th century.

Ivan the Terrible's Praying Seat (or Monomakh's Throne).

Of special interest is Ivan the Terrible's wooden carved praying-seat, otherwise known as «Monomakh's Throne», at the Cathedral's southern wall, opposite the iconostasis. The throne was installed here in 1551, four years after Ivan the Terrible was crowned for czardom. The throne's upper part is a marquee propped on four carved pillars; the marquee is adorned with kokoshniks covered with filigree carving. On the throne's three sides, there are carved inscriptions and low-relief pictures illustrating the text

Czar Ivan IV and Metropolitan Pilipp. Painting by R. Kuzmin.

A high-relief composition on Ivan the Terrible's Praying Seat.

of «The Tales of Princes of Vladimir». The central motif of the plot is the transfer of the symbols of state power and royal regalia, Byzantine Emperor Constantine's hat and scepter, from Byzantium to Russia. This very story gave the czar's throne its name. The idea of the continuity of power from Byzantine emperors via Kiev and Vladimir princes over to Moscow princes gained popularity in mid-16th century, an era of the consolidation of the czar's power. In the twelve margins on the throne's sides, the key episodes of the legend are reproduced.

Adjacent to the throne, the white-stone Patriarch's seat (late 15th century) stands near a pillar. At the neighboring pillar, in front of the altar, czarinas and princesses' praying seat of the 17th century is located. Like Ivan the Terrible's throne, it has a marquee-like top. Its inner side's lining is adorned with the Russian Empire's embroidered state emblem, the double-headed eagle bearing on its wings the emblems of Russian cities: Vladimir, Novgorod, Oryol, Astrakhan, Kazan and others; on its chest, the emblem of Moscow is fixed: St. George the Victor encircled with the chain of the Order of Andrei First Summoned, Russia's supreme state decoration since late 17th century.

Another fine work of applied art kept at the Assumption Cathedral is a copper marquee cast in 1624 «by the casting workshop's overseer» Dmitry Sverchkov, upon the request of Czar Mikhail Feodorovich. Located in the southwestern corner of the Cathedral, it was used to keep sacred items in there. The cubic marquee is topped with a cornice decorated with filigree kokoshniks in its form and ornament similar to those on Monomakh's Throne. Its top is a four-faceted pyramid. The marquee's sides are a cast filigree grille made of intertwined herbs, sprouts and leaves. In the days of past, a thin micaceous plate was laid underneath the grille to emphasize filigree lightness of the casting. The sides are linked by figure poles in the corners. Inside the marquee,

The Patriarch's seat

Czarinas' praying seat (left) and embroidered double-headed eagle with the coats of arms of Russian cities adorning the praying seat (right).

The copper marquee. D. Sverchkov. 1624. Right – the marquee's grille. Fragment.

a reliquary with the remains of Patriarch Germogen, one of the Russian Orthodox Church's most revered saints, is kept. He died in 1612, in a prison cell of the Moscow Kremlin's Chudov Monastery, forced by the Polish invaders to starve to death.

For many centuries, the Cathedral and the treasures of art it housed suffered much from fires and enemies. It was barbarously ransacked and devastated during the 1812 Patriotic War when the Kremlin was seized by Napoleon's army. 325 *poods* (pood = 16 kilograms) of silver and 18 poods of gold were stolen from the Cathedral. After the French intruders were driven out from the Russian capital massive renovation work was begun in the Cathedral. At that time, they hung in the Cathedral the big silver candelarium «Harvest» with a sheaf-of-wheat-shaped top. Curiously, it was made of 328 kg of silver that the Cossacks recaptured from the French convoy retreating from Moscow in December of 1812. The iconostasis was decorated with the new icon-frames reproducing the lost original ones. In early 20th century, ahead of the celebration of the 300th anniversary of the Romanov dynasty yet another large-scale renovation project was completed in the Cathedral. Then, the white tombstones over the Metropolitans' graves were put into metal boxes under glass covers made by the Ivan Khlebnikov Company, and bronze iconostases were erected at the walls.

The cross on the Cathedral's northern fa_ade erected on the site of Metropolitan Jonah's original burial place.

At the northern, southern and western walls of the Cathedral, tombs of the Russian religious leaders – Metropolitans and Patriarchs – are located. The most ancient among them is the tomb of Metropolitan Peter (died in 1326), in the Peter and Paul Chapel's altar. Near Metropolitan Peter's tomb, his successor Metropolitan Pheognost was buried. Pheognost transferred in 1339 his residence from Vladimir to Moscow for good, which move only reinforced the political prestige of Moscow Princes. In the Cathedral's southwestern corner, near the copper marquee, were buried Metropolitans Kiprian and Fotiy who headed the Russian Orthodox Church in late 14–early 15th century. In the northwestern corner, under the silver canopy (made in the early 19th century) stands the reliquary with the remains of Jonah, one of the first Metropolitans to be elected by the Russian

Patriarch Germogen. Picture from «The Czar's Title-book». 1672.

bishops' council (1448). Metropolitan Makary who headed the Russian Orthodox Church from the mid-16th century is buried at the northern wall. By the Cathedral's southern gate, under a metal canopy, Metropolitan Philipp's reliquary is located. For his public denunciation of Ivan the Terrible's cruel domestic policy (the so-called oprichnina) in 1568, he was ousted and exiled to a remote monastery, where soon was strangulated, upon Ivan's order, by Malyuta Skuratov. Philipp's remains were brought to the Cathedral in 1652, under Czar Alexei Mikhailovich's instruction.

Candelarium «Harvest».

Metropolitan Jonah's reliquary.

Along the Cathedral's southern and western walls, Patriarchs and heads of the Autocephalous Church are buried. The Russian Orthodox Church was made autonomous in late 16th century. Its first Patriarch Job, an adherent of Boris Godunov, was appointed in 1589. Side by side with him, Patriarch Filaret is buried, the father of Czar Mikhail Feodorovich, the first in the Romanov dynasty.

The last, tenth, Patriarch Adrian was buried at the western gate in 1700. Upon Emperor Peter the Great's order, the Patriarchate was abolished in 1703, and henceforth the Holy Synod headed the Russian Orthodox Church. Out of ten Patriarchs, nine were buried in the Cathedral. The grave of Nikon who was dethroned in 1667 is located in the Voskresensky Monastery in New Jerusalem outside Moscow. Interestingly, Czar Feodor Alexeyevich bestowed on the ousted Nikon his Patriarchal title, upon his request.

THE ANNUNCIATION CATHEDRAL

In the south-western corner of Cathedral Square, side by side with the Kremlin's Large Palace, stands a small nine-domed Annunciation Cathedral, a home church of Old Russian Great Princes and Czars, where wedding and baptism rituals were conducted. In the late 14th century, a small one-domed Annunciation Church stood here. Where the Kremlin's Large Palace stands today, once there was the Great Prince's palace connected by a passage with that church. In 1405, the Church was decorated with frescoes. According to the chronicle, Pheofan the Greek, Andrei Rublev, Prokhor from Gorodets, painted it.

By 1482, the old Church of Annunciation was largely decrepit, and Prince Ivan III decided to have a new one. The old building was dismantled, and the new cathedral was eventually erected upon the old foundation. The construction work lasted from 1484 to 1489. The new cathedral was crowned with three cupolas surrounded with a gulbishche – an open gallery with stairs leading down to Cathedral Square. The Cathedral was badly damaged in the big fire of 1547. During the reconstruction work, the gallery was covered with a vaulted ceiling, and small one-domed chapels were attached to the four corners. Then two more domes above the Cathedral's central part on the western side were erected. So, it had come to be nine-domed. At that time, the cupolas and the roof were covered with gilt copper, and the Cathedral was nicknamed «gold-topped». In 1572, a porch adorned with white-stone carvings, was attached to the Cathedral on the south-eastern side, and the chapel on the southern side was made Ivan the Terrible's personal praying place.

The Annunciation Cathedral. Postcard. Late 19th century.

The Annunciation Cathedral suffered much damage after Napoleon's invasion in 1812. In the times of Nicholas I and Alexander II, its nine cupolas were gilded anew, and today they are looming large among all the Kremlin's cupolas.

Once connected by a roofed passage with the Kremlin's Large Palace, the Annunciation Cathedral has always had the meaning of the main palatial church. From 15th century on, the Annunciation Cathedral's archpriests were Russian czars' spiritual fathers. The would-be czars visited the Cathedral on the coronation days and worshipped for the holy relics there. Following the ancient custom, the kliros was the place where the czarina and czarevich stood during services, while the czar prayed down below.

The Annunciation Cathedral's cupolas.

The western walls' frescoes.

The northern portal (below left) and a margin from the door's side.

At present, visitors enter the Cathedral-museum via the northern porch. Just take a look at the magnificent image of Veronica over the gate. Art historians believe the fresco was painted in 1661 by the leader of the royal team of icon-makers Simon Ushakov who rendered the conventional plot in the 17th-century new light-and-shade technique.

The Cathedral's central section can be accessed through the two carved white-stone portals covered with fine vegetation ornaments and painted in gold and azure (16th century); however, you can go only through the western gate, as the portal in the northern gallery is closed. Very interesting are the two-sided copper gates of the portals. They both are dated back to the 16th century, and by technique are akin to the southern gate of the Assumption Cathedral. On the northern gate, besides the «Annunciation» composition in the upper part of the sides, you can see the faces of Antique poets and philosophers. All the figurative compositions and ornaments were done using a rare technique of the so-called «fire gilding».

The Cathedral's central section is rather small, as the Great Princes' home church was meant to be used by only the members of the royal family. In the western corner, the kliros is located where a staircase leads hidden inside the southern and western thick walls. One of the Cathedral's notable sights is the tiled floor made of agate-like jasper that was transferred here from the city cathedral of Rostov Velikiy in the mid-16th century.

The key highlight of the Cathedral is its unique five-tiered iconostasis, which is invaluable indeed. It features the icons made in 1405 by Pheofan the Greek and Andrei Rublev. The iconostasis' uppermost tier consists of the icons showing half-length images of the Biblical patriarchs dated back to the second half of the 16th century; the second upper tier shows the prophets painted by Pskov icon-makers who restored the wall paintings after the 1547 big fire. The third upper

«The Savior Almighty» and «John the Precursor» (right). Phephan the Greek. Late 14th century.

«Our Lady». Phephan the Greek. Late 14th century.

The Annunciation Cathedral's iconostasis. Central section.

John the Zlatoust (left). Apostle Paul (right). Pheopan the Greek. Late 14th century.

Apostle Peter. Detail. Late 14th century.

«The Four-parted» icon. 1547–1551.

Archangel Michael. Late 14th century.

tier is called «the festive» (or «festivity»), because the 15 icons feature main Orthodox holidays that mark the key moments of Jesus Christ's earthly life. The seven icons on the left, save the fourth one, may have been painted by Andrei Rublev. The fourth icon in the «festive» tier, «Prepolove-niye» (dedicated to an Orthodox holiday commemorating the day when Jesus entered the church and began teaching) was painted by a 16th century unknown artist. The rest of the icons in this tier were painted by an unknown artist, presumably, Prokhor form Gorodets. The most memorable icon is «Laying in the Coffin» (the fifth on the right).

Below the festive tier, the deesis tier is located. The Greek word «deesis» means «worship». The deesis row of icons is an embodiment of the prayer for salvation. The icons here, which are dated back to the late 14th century, were presumably painted by an outstanding master Pheofan the Greek (except the icons showing Archangel Michael and Apostle Peter). In the middle of the monumental composition of nine icons, Jesus Christ is depicted in the white garment, sitting on the throne.

Of special interest are the examples of the Old Russian and Byzantine painting in the lowest, or the so-called «local», tier. Among them stands out «Our Lady of Odigitry» and the oldest icon «The Savior on the Throne». The inscription running along the low margin of the icon (it was added to the icon somewhat later) says it was paint-

ed in 1337 by icon-maker Mikhail. Who worked at Ivan Kalita's court. Beside it, you can see the cathedral's main icon «The Annunciation of Ustyug with Margins of Acathistus». Its central part is a 17th century copy of the famous 12th century icon (now featured in the Tretyakov Gallery) that was taken by Ivan the Terrible from Novgorod. Twenty four margins around the icon's central part illustrate the Acathistus, a religious hymn celebrating Virgin Mary.

To the right of the Annunciation, an icon depicting three saints: John the Baptist, Apostle Peter and Alexiy, the Man of God, is located. The two images were painted in 1683, whereas the third one, the namesake of Czar Alexei Mikhailovich, was added in the mid-18th century. The last icon on the right side of the local tier is «The Savior of Smolensk with Worshipping Saints Sergei of Radonezh and Varlaam of Khutyn», painted in the 16th century. In the middle, you can see Christ holding the Gospel in his left hand, while as if inviting us by his right hand to a silent soliloquy. On the left, beside Christ's feet, Sergei Radonezhskiy, the founder of the Trinity-St. Sergius Monastery outside Moscow, is depicted.

The iconostasis' silver king's gate was made in 1818 instead of the one lost after Napoleon's invasion. The iconostasis' frame of chased gilt brass and adorned with vegetation ornaments was made in the late 19th century. To the left of the king's

Icon «Annunciation of Ustyug with Acathistus» and its margins.

gate, you can see a 15th century icon «Our Lady of Smolensk-Shuyisk», in the late 17th–early 18th century painted frame showing the righteous women and prophetesses. On its left, there is «Savior on the Throne, with Our Lady and John the Baptist Worshipping for Him» (late 17th century). On the icon-doors (early 17th century) leading into the altar, archangels Uriel (left) and Raphael (right) are depicted. An icon «Nicholas the Miracle-Maker with Margins Showing Wonders» (on the northern wall, to the left of the iconostasis) was painted in 1699 by Feodor Ukhtomsky.

The Cathedral's wall painting is unique in its kind. We know that the Annunciation Cathedral was first painted in 1508 by a team of artists led by Feodosiy, the son of the renowned icon-maker Dionysy. The wall painting was badly damaged in the 1547 fire and was renovated later. The present-day frescoes in the Cathedral's central section were made in 1547–1551 and in the 17th–19th century were repeatedly restored. The frescoes have lost the initial brightness of color, but the elegant outlines and the strict composition reflect the icon-painters' fine craftsmanship. Here, you can find the themes that are traditional in the Old Russian painting, as well as new ones, characteristic of the 16th century. In the central cupola, you can see «Savior Almighty»; below, in the drum, the Evangelists; Our Lady and Jahveh are depicted in the two other cupolas. The themes of festivities and Gospel parables are rendered in the paintings on the walls' lunettes, the vaults, the credence's sides and the pillars.

Another theme popular in the late 15th–16th century, that of the Russian sovereigns' genealogy, of the continuity of power from Moscow up to Constantinople, is reflected in the paintings of the Cathedral's central part. On the pillars and the protrusions dividing the gallery's walls, you can see the images of the Moscow princes.

After having seen the central section, go into the Cathedral's southern gallery through

«Angels Ejecting Sinners». The southern vault's painting under the kliros. Detail.

«The Souls of the Righteous Before the Shrine». The southern wall's painting.

«Apocalypse». The western wall's painting.

the white portal to the right of the iconostasis. Recently, this stately portal's original look was restored, with the typical 15th century décor. The southern gallery's ancient frescoes did not survive, and A. Malakhov made the present-day oil paintings in 1836. In the southern gallery, you can see the 14–16th

«John the Precursor». 1560s.

century icons mostly painted by Moscow icon-makers especially for the Cathedral. Opposite the entrance, on the southern porch, stands a small iconostasis from the Archangel Gabriel Chapel, a unique example of the 16th century icon painting. To the left of the entrance, there are two large icons showing martyrs Dmitry Solunsky and Georgy (late 14th century). In the showcases, you can see several remarkable works of Old Russian icon-painting dedicated to the Holy Virgin, including «Our Lady of Tenderness of Yakhroma» (14th century), «Our Lady of Smolensk» (late 15th century),

The iconostasis from the Archangel Gabriel Chapel.

«Our Lady of Yakhroma». 14th century.

«Our Lady Odigitry» by a 14th century Byzantine artist. Take a look at the two 16th century crosses in the showcases to the right of the entrance. These are so-called behind-the-throne crosses, i. e. they stood inside the altar behind the throne. During holiday processions they were taken out to Cathedral Square together with icons and other relics. In between the crosses in the showcase, there is a large icon «John the Baptist» painted in the 1560s. Its yellow-brown and dark-

«Our Lady of Smolensk». 1470s.

green colors go in harmony with the silver-gilt frame. This icon was often exhibited abroad at major expositions of the Old Russian art.

Leaving the southern gallery, you find yourself again in the western gallery. Over the door, you can see the 16th century a fresco «The Feats of Monastic Hermits» showing the monks voluntarily suffering ordeals to absolve their sins. Of special interest is a monumental composition «The Trinity» (16th century), which, luckily, has been preserved far better than other paintings in the galleries, as it was put in the 18th century inside a silver holder. On the same wall, to the left, you can see the 16th century composition «Of Thee Rejoices» (renovated in the 19th century) dedicated to Our Lady. «The Annunciation» scene was painted in the 19th century over a filled gap.

Once in the northern gallery, take notice of the 16th century wall painting «The Wonder with Prophet Jonah» (to the right of the portal) based on the Biblical story about Jonah and the whale. Do pay your attention to the painted «portraits» of Antique philosophers, poets, playwrights and historians: Plato, Aristotle, Ptolemy, Plutarch, Homer with a wreath on his head, Virgil in a fedora hat and a red robe. In the Old Russia, they were considered the predecessors of the Christian wise men. Interestingly, some of them are dressed in Old Russian garb. They hold in their hands scrolls with inscriptions of philosophical maxims and moral teachings of the 16th century. Thus, Plato holds a scroll with a motto: «Ye must hope that Almighty Himself will send the heavenly teacher and tutor to people»; Socrates holds the scroll saying: «A good man is immune to any evil. Our soul is immortal; after death, the kind will be rewarded, the evil ones punished».

The Annunciation Cathedral's cross. Left: fragment.

The northern gallery.

The vaulted ceilings of the northern and western galleries are adorned with the 16th century multi-figu-re composition «The Tree of Jesse», Jesus Christ's genealogy. The fresco, an intricate ornament made of boughs and grape vines, begins in the northern gallery, where in the ceiling's central part main representatives of the kin are depicted: Jesse, David and Solomon. The genealogical tree is completed in the western gallery by the picture of Virgin Mary with Christ in her arms.

THE ARCHANGEL'S CATHEDRAL

In the southwestern corner of Cathedral Square, the five-domed Archangel's Cathedral proudly stands. A legend has it that in the 12th century, a wooden church built in the name of Archangel Michael, the leader of the heavenly host and the guardian of Russian princes, stood on this site. In 1333, upon Prince Ivan Kalita's order, the dilapidated church was demolished, and a new white-stone cathedral in the name of Archangel Michael was erected instead to commemorate Moscow's liberation from the terrible famine. It that was the then biggest in Moscow, as the chronicle asserts.

In 1340, Great Prince Ivan Kalita was buried in the new church, and after that, it came to be Russia's first state necropolis, where Moscow Great Princes and their close relatives, independent regional princes, found their lasting peace. The Moscow Great Prince Ivan III, who assumed the title of «the sovereign of All Russia», decided to rebuild the family necropolis. The dilapidated cathedral was dismantled, and eventually, in 1505–1508, the present-day Archangel's Cathedral was erected instead of it. An Italian architect, who was known in Russia under the name of Aleviz Noviy, was specially invited to Moscow from Venice to supervise the construction project. That is why on the outside, the Archangel's Cathedral looks very much like a Venetian palazzo. Also, well recognizable elements of Renaissance architecture were used in its décor. However, its design is quite typical of the Old Russian architecture. Its is a five-domed and six-poled cross-and-cupola cathedral, with narrow slot-like windows, a four-story side-building on the western side, where

The Cathedral's original look. Reconstruction by V. Merkelova.

The Archangel's Cathedral. Photograph. Late 19th century.

side-entrances lead to and where the kliros is located on the third-floor level. The five cupolas topping the Cathedral are somewhat shifted eastward, the drums are of different diameter and stand asymmetrically, thus giving an impression of dynamism and looseness of the architectural design. The Cathedral's veritable decoration is the fine stone carving.

The Archangel's Cathedral. Miniature from «The Book about the Election and Crowning for Reigning of Great Sovereign Czar and great Prince Mikhail Romanov».1672–1673.

For over its almost five-century history, the Archangel's Cathedral has changed considerably. Thus, the roofed galleries, where the distinguished guests and spectators gathered during religious processions and ceremonies held in Cathedral Square, have not survived. Its original magnificent iconostasis with precious-stone framed icons did not survive, either.

The Cathedral was first painted in 1564–1565, in the time of Ivan the Terrible, after the big fire of 1547. Details of the original wall painting have been preserved in the altar and on the altar's partition. The present-day painting in the cathedral's central section dates back to the mid-17th century. In 1652, four official icon-makers, Simon Ushakov, Stepan Ryazanets, Yakov Kazanets and Sidor Pospeyev, made excellent «removals», i. e. penciled copies of the second half of the 16th century painting.

The western portal – the gateway to the Cathedral; Right: Wall-painting. Detail.

In 1666, they painted the Cathedral anew with distemper on dry stucco.

The Great Prince's main Cathedral was dedicated to the works of Archangel Michael, who was revered as Moscow Princes' guardian angel in the times of war. The paintings on the northern and southern walls are dedicated to the works of Archangel Michael, the leader of the heavenly host and the protector of the oppressed. Of special interest are the battlefield scenes covering the Cathedral's southern and northern walls. These scenes are filled with a pathetic sense of fighting and triumph, and the mythological themes often referred to actual historical episodes. Thus, a fresco «Seizure of Jericho», in which Archangel Michael appears before Joshua and predicts him a victory, reminded about the

The Archangel's Cathedral's altar.

«The Annunciation» and «Christ's Nativity». The central vault's painting.

The southern wall's painting. Fragment «A Miracle of Gold».

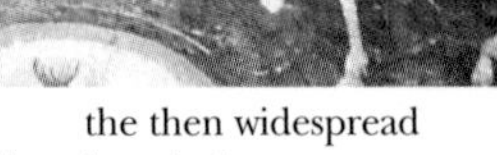

The northern wall's painting: «Archangel Michael Appears before Emperor Konstantin».

recent conquest of the Kazan Khanate that the Old Russians likened to the ancient Jericho. Another fresco on the southern wall «Gideon defeats the Midianites» indirectly refers to the recent Russian history that was rich in combat exploits. In particular, an onlooker is attracted to the archangel raising his sword over the enemies. The contemporaries of Ivan the Terrible saw in the Biblical story of the Midianites' defeat a paraphrase of the Russians' victory over the Tartar-Mongol army. The paintings in the Cathedral's western part (opposite the iconostasis) illustrate the key tenets of the Christian belief – «The Creed of Faith», aimed against the then widespread heretical movements.

The key component of the cathedral's interior is the magnificent iconostasis. Its wooden carved framework was made in 1679–1680 by Russian carvers. The twisted columns are adorned with ornamental grapes, bunches of fruits and leaves. Initially, the iconostasis was painted in different colors, gilded and silvered. When under the 1853 restoration, it was gilded through and through. Exceptionally beautiful is the king's gate, with its carved filigree canopy, where an icon «The Last Supper» is fixed. The icons on the sides of the gate, Evangelists and «The Annunciation» were painted not on wooden boards, but metal ones. In the two upper tiers, the prophets and the deesis, the 17th century icons hang, some of them are still stained by later painted-on images. The festive icons were made in 1679–1680. Thanks to the archival documents, it is known that the outstanding 17th century official icon-maker Feodor Zubov painted icons «Savior on the Throne» and «Our Lady» (the second upper tier, center). Together with Mikhail Milyutin he painted a composition «Crucifixion with Worshipping Our Lady and John the Theologian» topping the iconostasis. Icons in the lower tier date back to different eras: «Our Lady with the Infant» and «Christ the Almighty», to the 17th century; «The Annunciation of Ustyug» (the second one, left of the king's gate), to the 16th century.

«Archangel Michael» (the second one, right of the king's gate)

Icon «Archangel Michael» with his acts.

The Cathedral's iconostasis.

Icon «Annunciation of Ustyug». 16th century. Above: Detail.

is one of the most famous works of Old Russian painting. According to a legend, it was made in late 14th– early 15th century upon the order of Great Princess Eudokia, the widow of Dmitry Donskoi, in commemoration of her husband and his victory in the Kulikovo Field, and was devised for the Palace's Church of Our Lady's Nativity. Later, it became the main icon of the 14th century-built Archangel's Cathedral, and was moved from there into the present-day building.

The Cathedral's wall painting is unique in featuring over 60 actual historical persons on its poles and in the lower tiers of the walls. Historians believe, Ivan the Terrible's closest aides sanctioned the plots and themes of the frescoes. One of the then key themes was the idea of the continuity of power from Byzantine emperors via Kiev and Vladimir princes over to Moscow princes. That is why you can see on the pillars the images of Kiev Princess Olga and Kiev Prince Vladimir (the eastern facet of the north-eastern pillar and the western facet of the northwestern pillar), Vladimir Prince Andrei Bogolyubsky (the northern facet of the southeastern pillar, the first row), Alexander Nevsky (the northern facet of the southwestern pillar, the first row), as well as his son, Moscow Prince Daniil Alexandrovich (the southern facet of the northwestern pillar, the first row). The idea of the continuity of power from Byzantium had taken root in the Russian political thought as early as in the 15th century, and that is why Byzantine Emperor Michael III Paleolog is depicted in the first row of the southeastern pillar's western facet. The grandmother of Czar Ivan the Terrible, Sophia Paleolog, deemed herself his descendant.

As the Archangel's Cathedral had been until the early 18th century the Russian Great Princes and Czars' burial place, its wall paintings reflect its special function. The lower rows on the northern, western and southern walls feature a gallery of images of great and independent princes, from Ivan Kalita to Vassiliy III buried in the Cathedral (25 tombs were transferred in here from the 14th century cathedral). However, these are not portraits, in the proper sense, but, according to a chronicler, «likenesses of the Princes». Only the lavish garments and the regalia were depicted true to life.

«Christ the Archpriest». The iconostasis' local tier.

«Lazarus' Resurrection». The iconostasis' festive tier.

The tombs of Czars Feodor Alexeyevich and Ivan Alexeyevich.

The reliquary with Czarevich Dmitry's relics.

Only males were buried in the Cathedral. Their remains rest in white-stone coffins 1.5 meters below the surface. In the Archangel's Cathedral's necropolis, there are 54 tombs, of which 52 are beneath the floor's stone plates and 2 reliquaries stand on the floor: one, with the remains of Mikhail Chernigovsky murdered in the Golden Horde in 1245, in the altar, and the other, with the remains of czarevich Dimitry, Ivan the Terrible's youngest son canonized in 1605, in the cathedral's central nave.

In the 17th century, 46 tombstones were fixed over the tombs. There are only 46 stones because sometimes they were put over two or even three tombs. The white-stone plates on the front side, covered with Old Slav ligature, are adorned with carved vegetation ornaments. During the renovation works timed with the 300th anniversary of he Romanov dynasty, the tombstones were put into glass showcases.

The majority of the tombs at the southern wall (to the right of the iconostasis) dates back to the era of unification of separate Russian principalities for the sake of fighting the Golden Horde's Tartar-Mongol invaders. Moscow Prince Ivan Kalita's tomb (1341), the nearest to the Cathedral's southern entrance, stands in the first row at the wall. Over it, there is the «portrait» of the Prince, «the gatherer of the Russian lands». His sons, Simeon Gordiy (Proud) and Ivan Krasniy (Red) who continued to pursue their father's policy, are buried beside, their «portraits» fixed over their tombstones. In the next row (a tombstone in the middle), you can see the grave of Ivan Kalita's grandson Dmitry Ivanovich Donskoi who led the Old Russian principalities in their open offensive against the Golden Horde. The triumphant Battle on the Kulikovo Field on Sept. 8, 1380, marked the first victory of the Russian army over the Tartar-Mongol invaders.

Another group of tombs is dated back to the formative era of the centralized Russian state and of the consolidation of power of Moscow Great Princes (the 15–16th century). At the Cathedral's southern wall, on a podium in front of the iconostasis, you can find the tombs of Great Princes Vassiliy II, Ivan III and Vassiliy III, the great-grandfather, grandfather and father of Czar Ivan the Terrible.

Ivan IV, the Terrible, who was the first among Moscow Great Princes granted the title of «the czar and sovereign ruler», assumed he was eligible for a special burial place. Upon his order, a special czar's burial site was created in the southern corner of the Cathedral's altar part. However, Ivan IV's elder son Ivan was the first to be buried there, after his father killed him with his staff during their quarrel. Eventually, Ivan the Terrible and his son Feodor Ioannovich, the last Russian czar of the Ryurikovich dynasty, were buried here. The reliquary with the remains of czarevich Dmitry holds a special place in the cathedral's necropolis. Dmitry died in the town of Uglich under mysterious circumstances. In 1606, his remains were moved from Uglich to the Kremlin's Archangels' Cathedral. A lid with the punched full-length image of Czarevich Dmitry initially covered the reliquary. Later, a carved white-stone canopy was erected over the reliquary.

A number of tombs in the Cathedral's north-western corner are dated back to the time of Ivan the Terrible, including those of Princes Staristky, of the powerful clan that opposed the Czar's neutrality policy. The dissident princes were executed; however, they were honored to be buried in the Archangel's Cathedral as was becoming to their princely status. Inside the altar part, in the John the Precursor's Chapel, an early 17th century famous commander Prince Mikhail Skopin-Shuisky is bu-

The southern wall's painting (right).

White-stone carve-work adorning the Cathedral's tombs.

The western wall's painting. Detail.

ried. The «boyars' czar» Vassiliy Shuisky buried near the Archangel's Cathedral's north-western pillar was yet another great man of state of the «troubled times». He died in 1612 when in the Polish captivity, and in 1635, his remains were transferred to the Cathedral's necropolis.

«The Dying Man Saying Goodbye to His Family». Fresco in the sacristy. 16th century.

The tombs of Ivan IV and his sons Ivan and Feodor in the Cathedral's sacristy.

The Cathedral's sacristy. Entrance to the John the Precursor's Chapel.

At the southeastern pillar, the first czars of the Romanov dynasty are buried: Mikhail Feodorovich (1596–1645) and Alexei Mikhailovich (1629–1676), the father of Czar Peter I, and their juvenile sons. At the northeastern pillar, Alexei Mikhailovich's two sons are buried, the brothers of Peter I, Czars Feodor (1661–1682) and Ivan V (1666–1696).

By the way, there was an interesting custom observed until the early 17th century. Visitors left on the tombs of Russian sovereigns request notes, and reigning czars took the notes when visiting the Cathedral. Czars visited the Cathedral often, and some visits were of ritualistic nature. Thus, after coronation ceremonies in the Assumption Cathedral, Russian czars would go to the Archangel's Cathedral to pray before the tombs of their ancestors. Czars would come to the Cathedral before leaving for another war, as if asking the ancestors for their blessing. Besides, Russians monarchs visited the Cathedral during the Passion Week and on Easter Day.

After the Russian capital was moved from Moscow to St. Petersburg in the early 18th century, nobody was buried in the Archangel's Cathedral. One exception was the burial of a 15-year-old Emperor Peter II, the grandson of Peter I, who died of smallpox in Moscow in 1730. His grave is located at the northeastern pillar. The new imperial necropolis was created in the Peter and Paul Cathedral in St. Petersburg.

THE CHURCH OF LAYING OUR LADY'S HOLY ROBE

A few steps away from Assumption Cathedral, stands the Church of Laying our Lady's Holy Robe, a small one-dome cathedral built in 1484 in the Metropolitan's (later, Patriarch's) estate in the Kremlin.

The Church's iconostasis. 1627.

«Archangel Gabriel». Nazary Istomin. 1627.

According to the chronicle, back in 1450, Moscow Metropolitan Jonah laid the first brick of «a stone chamber in front of the Our Holy Lady's Gate and a church in the name of Laying the Fair Robe of Our Holy Lady». A legend has it that the construction of this church in the Kremlin was related to a glorious victory over an enemy. In 1451, a Tartar prince Mazovsha came to besiege Moscow with a big army. A cruel battle was going on under the city's walls for almost whole day. The enemy encircled the Kremlin but failed to seize the fortress. After a frightening night, the Muscovites, well prepared for a new assault, found out in the morning that the enemy had left. The legend states it was due to Our Lady's protection, especially as it happened on the holiday of Laying Our Lady's Holy Robe. So, the construction of the Church of Laying Our Lady's Holy Robe was related to the «pending liberation from the Tartars' yoke» (as the events were called in the chronicle).

The Church was named after the Orthodox holiday of Laying Our Lady's Holy Robe, or Rizpolozheniye. According to an Orthodox tale, Virgin Mary's robe was taken from Palestine to Constantinople in the 5th century and laid in the Church of Our Lady in Vlakherny to be kept there for good. (Vlakherny is located in western Constantinople). From then on, the 15th of July, was widely celebrated by all Christians. After Russia was converted to Christianity in the late 10th century, the holiday began to be observed by the Russian Orthodox Church, too.

«Laying Our Lady's Holy Robe». First half of the 17th century.

The 1473 Kremlin's big fire devastated the Metropolitan's estate and all the buildings. Upon Metropolitan Geronty's order, a new church, in its present-day design, was built in 1474–5 by Pskov's stonelayers. This small brick edifice is as if thrusting upwards. The impression is reinforced by a high *podklet* (ground floor) where the Metropolitan's treasury must have been kept, and the high drum with narrow windows topped with the Old Russian helmet-like gilt cupola. Diminutiveness and elegance of this church is highlighted by its contrast to the monumental forms of the neighboring Assumption Cathedral.

For quite a long time, the Cathedral had been Moscow Metropolitans' (from 1589 – Patriarchs') home church. In the mid-17th century Patriarch Nikon built a new palace for himself, with the home Church of the Twelve Apostles, and the Church of Laying Our Lady's Holy Robe was given over to the royal family, to the czarina and czarevnas. It was linked by a passage to their quarters; the female members of the Czar's family used its gallery to attend services in the Assumption Cathedral.

The entrance is located on the Church's eastern side. Walking upstairs, you will find yourself on a high gallery; from here, you can enter the Church's central section. It is not too spacious, but cozy, thanks to the well-balanced architectural proportions, wall paintings and the iconostasis, and the harmoniously matching colors. The four-tiered iconostasis has been preserved almost intact, except for the icons in the lower, or local, tier. It is one of the true masterpieces of the Russian art of the first half of the 17th century. The iconostasis

«The Trinity». Nazary Istomin. 1627.

Frescoes on the Church of Laying Our Lady's Holy Robe's western wall. Detail. Scenes from the Acathistus.

was made in 1627, upon Patriarch Filaret's order, by the Russian outstanding artist Nazary Istomin Savin. The iconostasis' composition is conventional. Up in the higher tier, are images of the prophets; below them, are the festivity icons, 12 of which depicting Christian holidays: The Annunciation, Christ's Nativity, The Purification, The Baptism, The Resurrection of Lazarus, Entry into Jerusalem, Christ's Transfiguration, The Crucifixion, The Descent into Hell, The Ascension, The Trinity, The Assumption. The deesis tier is in the central place, with the icon «Savior Almighty». Christ sits on a throne, holding the opened Gospel in his hand, in the sphere filled with cherubs and angels. On his left, are Our Lady, archangel Michael, apostle Peter, Prince Vassiliy the Great, Metropolitan Peter; on his right, are John the Baptist, archangel Gabriel, apostle Paul, St. John the Golden-tongued (Zlatoust), Metropolitan Jonah. The specific feature of this iconostasis is that it includes the images of Moscow's first holy fathers: Metropolitan Peter who moved his cathedra from Vladimir to Moscow, and Metropolitan Jonah who ordered to construct the Kremlin's first Church of Laying Our Lady's Holy Robe.

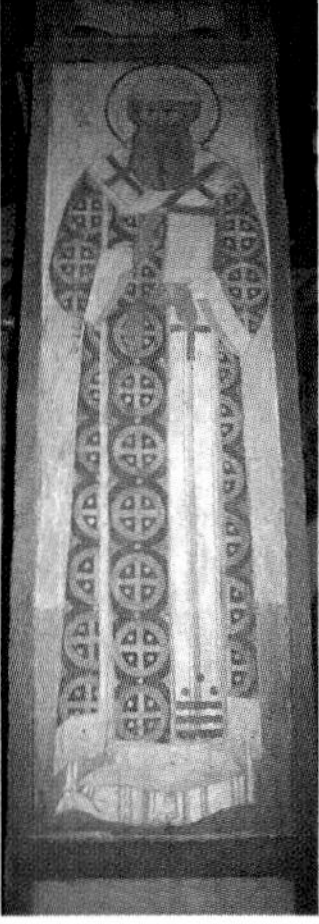

The north-western pole's painting.

«Laying Our Lady's Holy Robe». The northern wall's painting. Detail.

Two more Nazary Istomin's icons can be found in the local tier. To the left of the King's Gate, is «The Trinity» icon, whose composition can be traced back to the famous Andrei Rublev's Trinity. To the right of the King's Gate you can see the Church's main icon «Laying Our Lady's Robe» painted by an unknown artist in the first half of the 17th century. In it, the Vlakhernsky Cathedral is shown; in the foreground, you can see the Constantinople's Patriarch and the Byzantine Emperor near the throne, on which the golden casket with the Robe stands. On its the right hangs an icon «Our Lady of Tikhvin», in a silver frame (16th century) inserted into another frame with painted margins (17th century). Take a look at the King's Gate leading into the altar. The Gate dates back to the 16thg century, and was transferred here from the Kremlin's unpreserved Church of the Savior in the Bor. The marquee over the door and the upper part of its sides are fashioned like Old Russian women's headwear. On the sides, the Annunciation scene and the four Evangelists are painted; on the marquee, an icon «The Eucharist» features Christ giving the eucharist of wine and bread.

The southern wall's painting. Detail.

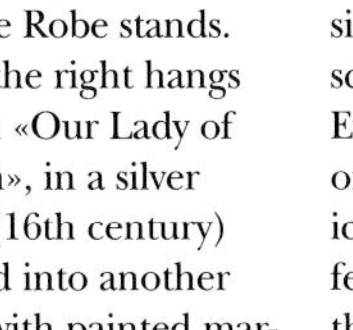

The surfaces of the walls, vaults and pillars are covered with paintings made in 1644 by royal icon-makers Sidor Pospeyev, Ivan Borisov (who contributed to the monumental artwork in the Assumption Cathedral) and Semyon Abramov. An interesting feature of the Church's wall painting is the absence of the Doomsday images on its western wall. Otherwise, the wall painting is quite conventional: in the central dome you can see the Savior Almighty; on the drum, the prophets and

The apside's composition

the evangelists. On the vaults and the adjacent lunettes, there are classical images.

The paintings on the southern, western and northern walls are dedicated to Virgin Mary. The two upper tiers of the southern and northern walls, the second tier of the western wall and small tub-shaped vaults of the Church are covered by 15 images of the proto-Evangelical cycle – a story about Mary's parents, about her life in her father's house, and her praying in the cathedral, about her marriage and giving birth to her son and her assumption. The two lower tiers are illustrations to the solemn chant in honor of Our Lady, Acathistus, created in Byzantium in the 6–7th century.

You have already seen the so-called «portraits» of the Russian men of state in the Archangels' and the Annunciation cathedrals. They symbolized the idea of the continuity of Great Princes' and Czars' power, as well as its heavenly origin. The familiar faces can be seen in the Church of Laying Our Lady's Holy Robe: the images of Kiev's Prince Vladimir (the upper tier on the southern pillar's eastern facet), Prince Alexander Nevsky (the western facet) and his son, Moscow Prince Dmitry Alexandrovich (the southern facet). In the lower tier (on the southern and eastern facets), you can see Russia's first saints Boris and Gleb, the sons of Kiev's Prince Vladimir Svyatoslavich. They died in 1015, fallen victims of the then ongo-

Nicholas of Mozhaisk. Moscow. Mid-17th century.

Wooden high-relief composition «The Crucifixion with the Robbers».

Our Lady of Passions. Moscow. Second half of the 17th century (right).

Savior Emmanuel, Nicholas the Wonder-worker and the Saints of Rostov Great. Late 16th century.

the gallery. Here, you can see the exposition of Russian wooden sculpture and carvings of the 14–17th century. Each exhibit is unique in itself and embodies the spirit of its time. There are very few large wooden sculpted figures left. Many of those perished in the numerous fires, some were destroyed deliberately, as the Russian Orthodox Church detected in them a pagan or Catholic influence.

The earliest work exhibited in the gallery is «George the Warrior»

A cross. The Russian North. 16th–17th century.

Cherub. The Solovetskiy Monastery. Second half of the 17th century.

ing feud, and in the 11th century were canonized. On the neighboring pillar are the images of Russian Metropolitans: in the upper tier, Peter, Alexiy, Jonah, Philipp I; in the lower, Kiprian, Fotiy, Geronty, and Philipp II.

After having seen the Church's central section, you can go via the western door into

dated back to the late 14th– early 15th century. Sculpted figures of saint warriors were a favorite topic of the Old Russian wood carvers. Ordinary people cherished those sculpted images as their guardians and protectors; these were the symbols of courage and bravery of the fighters with foes.

Nikola of Mozhaisk was believed to be a major guardian. In the late 14th century, the similar image of the saint – full length, in parade garment, holding a cathedral symbolizing the fortress of Mozhaisk in his left hand and a sword in his right hand, was hung over the gate of the fortress or Mozhaisk (outside Moscow).

The lid of Metropolitan Jonah's reliquary from the Assumption Cathedral is an interesting example of the 17th century Russian monumental plastic art. Jonah was an important historic figure. In 1448, a council of the Russian bishops elected him Metropolitan without prior consent of the Constantinople's Patriarch. This key decision laid the ground for the Russian Orthodox Church's autonomy from Constantinople.

On the gallery's walls and in the showcases, you can see carved wooden icons of the 16–17th century showing the most cherished images of Our Lady and saints: Paraskeva the Friday, St. George the Victor and Nikita the Martyr.

Of special interest are tiny icons and folders covered with filigree carvings. All these wonderful masterpieces were made by carvers from Moscow and other cities of European Russia.

THE IVAN THE GREAT BELL-TOWER

The Ivan the Great Bell-Tower complex closes Cathedral Square in the east and includes the Bell-Tower, the Zvonnitsa (belfry) and Filaret's Annex, or Filaret's Belfry. The space behind it has been called Ivanov Square from time immemorial.

The chronicle tells us that the Church of St. John Ladder-maker once stood here. It was built in the 15th century, upon Ivan Kalita's will. In 1505, a new church and a belfry were founded instead of it, in the name of the same saint. An Italian architect Bon Fryazin supervised the construction project. Three years later, the newly built bell-tower of about 60 m high (i. e. the two lower and a part of the third row of the present-day's tower) was named «Ivan the Great». From the top of the Ivan Bell-Tower, one could see the vistas around the Kremlin at a distance of 30 km; therefore, it was used as a watch-tower.

In 1598–1600, Czar Boris Godunov decided to erect in the Kremlin a grandiose cathedral, which, upon his design, would surpass all the Kremlin's cathedral and churches. To make the Bell-Tower congruent with the cyclopic cathedral-to-be, it was overbuilt up to the height of 81 m and topped with a golden dome. Below the dome, a gilt-lettered inscription against the blue background runs: «by the instruction of Great Sovereign, Czar and Great Prince Boris Feodorovich... and his son... Feodor Borisovich... the cathedral was built and gilded in the second summer of their rule, in 7108 (1600). Accurately cut white-stone blocks lie in the Bell-Tower's foundation and the powerful socle, whereas higher tiers are made of lighter brick. Its architectural design is simple: three long and narrowing eight-faceted pillars are put on top of each other, topped with a high drum carrying an elegant golden cupola and a 7-meter-high cross. Each eight-faceted pillar

Public festivities on Ivanov Square with the royal family's procession. Watercolor by V. Sadovnikov. 1851.

ends in an open arched gap, or «a ringing». Thanks to the gradual narrowing of the height and diameter of each, an onlooker gets an impression of the tower thrusting upwards. The John the Stair-Builder's Church was once located in the ground tier; above it, there were rooms of unknown purpose. These rooms are rather small, because the walls here are very thick, up to 5 m at their base and 2.5 m at the second tier. Inside the walls there is a stone stair that at the third tier is replaced by an iron one leading up into the cupola.

The in-wall staircase in the Bell-Tower's first tier.

A four-tiered annex topped with a golden cupola standing on a solid drum to the left of the Tower is the Uspenskaya Zvonnitsa (the Assumption Belfry), built by Petrok Maliy in 1532–43. In 1624, upon Patriarch Filaret's order, another belfry was erected. Built according to the design of architect Bazhen Ogurtsov, it had a marquee-like roof and was called Filaret's Annex. When retreating from Moscow in 1812, Napoleon ordered that the Ivan the Great Bell-Tower be blown up. The Zvonnitsa and Filaret's Annex were completely destroyed, the Bell-Tower was fractured in the upper tier, but stood firm. In 1814–15, both buildings were reconstructed by architects I. Yegotov and L. Rusk (design by I. Gilardi) almost in their original dimensions, with classic elements of décor added. In the late 19th century, the Zvonnitsa's rooms in the second and third tiers housed the Patriarch's sacristy and the Nicholas Gostunskiy Church.

The bells of Ivan the Great Bell-Tower, each of 21 ones being a true museum item, were mainly made by Russian casters in the 17–19th century. Six large bells are well visible in the gaps of the Bell-Tower's lower tier. If you look at them from Cathedral Square, the two bells closest to the Zvonnitsa were made in 1775 by Semyon Mozzhukhin. Both bells were recast from older ones broken in the 16th century, as the inscriptions on their bodies tell us. Each weighs over 7 ton. The third bell on the right is the Novgorodskiy, was recast in 1730 by the then famous caster Ivan Motorin from a 1556-

Below: left – the bells of the Ivan the Great's second tier; right – the gold-lettered inscription under the Bell-Tower's dome.

made bell of Novgorod's Sophia Cathedral. Its weight is about 7 ton. The Shirokiy (Broad) bell cast in 1679 by Vasiliy and Jakov Leontiyevs hangs close to the Novgorodskiy. It was given its appellation thanks to its unusual dimensions. As a rule, the Russian bells are of the same height and width; this one, however, has a 2-meter diameter, almost 30 cm more than its height. Its weight is 5 ton. The next bell, Slobodskiy, was recast in 1641 from the old one. The last in this row is the Rostovskiy bell cast in 1687 for a monastery near the city of Rostov, which was later transferred to Moscow. It was created by the 17th century famous caster Philipp Andreyev, who made the resonant bells of the Rostov Kremlin. In the second row, hang ten bells made in the 16–17th century. Two of them were cast by Feodor Motorin, the father of the famous Ivan Motorin who created the famous Czar Bell. Lastly, three minor bells made in the 17th century hang in the third row.

The most massive bells are fixed in the Uspenskaya Zvonnitsa. In the gap nearest to the Bell-Tower, you can see Reut, or Revun (Roarer), a cyclopic 32-ton bell cast in 1622 by Andrei Chokhov. In his long life, the Reut saw two dramatic events. In 1812, when the retreating French troops blew up the Zvonnitsa, it fell down but suffered little damage: only its «ears» were broken off. After the Zvonnitsa was restored, the bell was again fixed in its place. And in 1855, at the coronation service in honor of the newly crowned Emperor, Alexander II, the bell fell off its beam, broke through three wooden and two stone floors and killed several people. Luckily, the Reut survived, and it had been ringing for more thirty years. Yet another giant, the Uspenskiy bell (ca. 64 ton), looms large in the Belfry's central gap. It was cast in 1817 by a Moscow master Jakov Zavyalov and his assistant Rusinov from a bell broken

One of 7-ton bells cast by Semyon Mozzhukhin in 1775.

View from the Ivan the Great Bell-Tower on Red Square and the former Presidium of the USSR Supreme Soviet building.

in 1812 after the Bell-Tower was blown up. A 13-ton big bell cast in 1704 by Ivan Motorin hangs in Filaret's Annex. Unfortunately, it cannot be seen from the outside.

The bells have been always an important part of the Russians' daily life – on days of woe, of sorrow, and of joy, bells' ringing would herald the major events. The bells keep ringing in the Kremlin these days, too, on big religious holidays.

The Czar Bell and details of its décor.

Nowadays, the Zvonnitsa's lower level is an exhibition hall where items from the Kremlin's state museums are put on display: pieces of decorative and applied art and jewelry, precious fabrics, armaments, embroidery, and the like, from the Moscow Kremlin and Russia's other museums. If you have spare time, do spend a half-hour or so in this hall...

Bypassing the Ivan the Great on its left-hand side, you enter Ivanov Square. Here, you will see the two amazing masterpieces of the Russian casting – the Czar Bell and the Czar Cannon. In the 17th century, the State Departments Building stood on this square, and the department clerks while announcing the Czar's new decrees, yelled «across the whole Ivanov».

The making of the Czar Bell (the world's biggest one) continued the tradition of the Russian monumental casting. Back in the 16th century, Moscow casters made gigantic bells. Thus, in 1653, Yemeliyan Danilov made a bell of 8 thousand poods (128 ton), and in 1654, Alexander Grigoriyev cast the Big Uspenskiy bell of the same weight. However, these masterpieces of the art of bell casting have not survived. The Czar Bell, in this sense, is the unique example. On the 26th of July of 1730, Empress Anne Ioannovna issued a supreme decree on casting the new bell. In the Kremlin's territory, they dug out a huge 10-meter deep casting hole; four furnaces were set up around it. To cast a new bell, the casters took the pieces of an old 130-ton bell broken during the 1701 fire – it was an alloy of tin, bronze, silver and gold.

On the 26th of November of 1734, the casters embarked on the smelting process. Two hundred men participated in it. However, two days later, three furnaces went out of work and they had to suspend the process. Also, there were other obstacles. All of a sudden, the principal caster Ivan Motorin died, and his son Mikhail took over. At last, one year later, on the 25th of November of 1735, the bell was finally cast. According to the archival documents, the casting process took only 36 minutes; every minute, 6 ton of smelt metal was poured into the mould. The newly cast bell was 6.14 meter high, its diameter was 6.6 meter, and it weighed over 200 ton.

In the summer of 1736, the bell-makers started to cover the bell with chased adornment, which had not been completed. On the 29th of May, 1737, during a powerful fire in the Kremlin, the roof of a supporting structure erected over the casting hole fell down on the bell. When the burning debris was poured with cold water to extinguish the fire, the bell cracked due to the uneven cooling, and an 11.5-ton piece broke off.

Ivanov Square.

The injured giant had lain on the ground for 99 years. All the lifting projects were rejected due to high costs required. Only in 1836, architect and engineer Auguste Montferrant (who built the Isaac's Cathedral in St. Petersburg) raised the Czar Bell on a pedestal. The Bell has stood there until the present day.

Do pay attention to the splendid décor of the bell (sculptor Feodor Medvedev, master Peter Kokhtev, caster Peter Lukovnikov). On its side facing the Spasskiy Tower, Czar Alexei Mikhailovich is depicted symbolizing that the bell made in his time was recreated anew; over him, there are the images of Our Lady and John the Baptist. On the reverse side, there is the image of Empress Anne Ioannovna, who ordered the bell to be cast. Over her portrait, there are the images of Jesus, prophetess Anne, the Empress' patron saint, apostle Peter (Anne Ioannovna considered herself Emperor Peter the Great's successor). The texts in the medallions held by the angels tell the story of the bell's making, and on a margin underneath Anne Ioannovna's feet the names of casters Ivan and Mikhail Motorins are carved. The bell's body is adorned with vegetation ornament in the baroque style. The copper scepter with a gilt cross, which Montferrant designed, gives the finish to the monumental masterpiece.

The Czar Cannon and a detail of its décor.

The Czar Bell was restored in 1979–1980. Its surface was cleared of the layers of lacquer and paint, its base was repaired, and the splinter that had gone almost half a meter deep into the earth, was raised.

Together with the Czar Bell, the famous Czar Cannon was thoroughly renovated, too. The contemporary master casters reproduced the lacking elements of the plated cast ornament and the carriage, cleared the cannon's body of alien layers of paint and dirt, and lacquered the carriage, the gun tube and the cannonballs. So, take a few steps forwards down Ivanov Square and admire the Russian wonder-gun in its awesome and rather peaceful grandeur.

The world's biggest cannon was cast of high quality bronze in 1586 at Moscow's Cannon Court by Andrei Chokhov. The first artillery pieces that replaced the launching and wall-tumbling machines were first cast in Old Russia in the 14th century. In the time of Ivan the Terrible, cannons were used in military operations. First Russian cannons were cast by bellmakers; later, special cannon-casters' teams were organized.

The Czar Cannon is a unique item, indeed. The gun tube's weight is 40 ton, its length is 5.34 m, its caliber is 890 mm. Judging by the type of its gun tube, the Czar Cannon is a mortar. The cannon's surface is lavishly adorned with the vegetation ornament and inscriptions.

Eight cast staples are fixed on the tube's sides, whereby the cannon was moved. One of the inscriptions reads as follows: «Upon the instruction of the faithful and Christ-loving Czar and Great Prince Feodor Ioannovich, the sovereign ruler of all Great Russia... was cast this cannon in the renowned regal city of Moscow in the year of 7094, in the third summer of his reign. The cannon was made by cannon-caster Ondrei Chokhov».

Originally, the cannon was called «Russian Great Fowling-Piece», as it was designed to fire with pellets, or case shots. It then was given its present-day appellation thanks to its cyclopic size. The cannon was devised for the Kremlin's defense. However, not a single shot was fired from it. Initially, the Czar Cannon was fixed on Red Square near the Lobnoye Spot. At that time, the cannon lacked a carriage, and a special base was made for it. In the 18th century, it was moved into the Kremlin and fixed in the Arsenal's inner yard only to be moved again to its main gate.

In 1835, architect A. Bryullov cast the carriages for the Czar Cannon and other Kremlin's large guns in St. Petersburg according to

Above: the Kremlin's Garden is most beautiful in summertime.

A military parade in the Moscow Kremlin. Watercolor by V. Sadovnikov. 1851.

the sketch. Fixed on the carriage adorned with magnificent cast ornaments the Czar Cannon was put near the Armory Chamber's old building opposite the Arsenal. Four cast-iron cannonballs weighing ca. 1 ton each were laid at its base. In 1960, when the Palace of Congresses (now, the Kremlin's State Palace) was under construction, the Armory Chamber's old building (architect I. Yegotov) was dismantled. The cannons that stood near it were moved to the Arsenal, whereas the Czar Cannon was taken to its present-day location on Ivanov Square.

Crossing Ivanov Square, you will find yourself in the Kremlin's Garden laid out in 1940. By the way, gardens have been the Kremlin's main attraction since the days of old. Unfortunately, most of them have not been preserved. In the 17th century inventories, «upper» and «lower» gardens are mentioned, as well as «palatial» and «chamber» ones – at that time, gardens were an important part of the Kremlin's architecture and landscape. Often, they were «hanging gardens» – planted on the arched roofs. Thus, the Upper Garden was created on the roof of the Boris Godunov Palace. The Patriarch's Palace had it own «Upper Garden»: on a log platform, soil was strewn and salads, beans, peas, currant and gooseberry shrubs were planted. Later, the Patriarchs' gardeners grew tulips, poppies and other flower up there.

But, of course, much more popular were the so-called «lower gardens», i. e. laid out on the ground. Thus, in the 17th century, on the slopes of the Borovitskiy Hill, a big embankment garden was arranged. It was divided into the Upper and the Lower ones where not only the regular apple trees and currant and gooseberry shrubs, but even the then surprising grape vines were planted. In the late 19th century, the rather thick Kremlin's Lower Garden was a popular public ground where Kremlin residents would take a stroll. In 1879, the Tainitskiy Garden of ash-trees was created on the Borovitskiy Hill's southern slope, near the Tainitskaya Tower. In 1926, a small public garden was created between the Arsenal and the Senate building. In this little garden, a monument to the Kremlin's cadets killed in combat in 1920 was erected. The Winter Gardens in the Kremlin's Large Palace and the Kremlin's State Palace carry on the traditions of the Russian landscape architecture.

The Tainitskiy Garden and the Vodovzvodnaya Tower.

THE PATRIARCH'S PALACE

The Kremlin's last architectural memorial you are invited to visit is the Patriarch's Palace, or Patriarshiye Palaty. This is one of the rare examples of the 17th century civil architecture that has been preserved in the Kremlin's premises.

The Patriarch's Palace consists of the living quarters and the public quarters, with many rooms, narrow staircases, and passageways. The two-story western wing includes the parade Cross Chamber and the enfilade that connects the Patriarch's Palace with the Terem Palace. The four-story eastern wing of the Palace ends in a five-domed Church of the Twelve Apostles, which is incorporated into the main building.

No record of the earliest buildings in the Metropolitan's estate has survived. In the chronicles, there is only one remark about a «chamber» of Metropolitan Fotiy that dates back to the first quarter of the 15th century. Metropolitan of Moscow and all Russia Jonah was first to encourage his builders to erect stone structures. According to the chronicle, upon his order in 1450, «a stone chamber in front of Our Holy Lady's doors, as well as a home church in the name of Our Holy Lady's Fair Holy Robe were begun to be built». This is one of the earliest references to a stone housing project in the Kremlin.

The southern façade's décor. Fragment.

The terrible fires that often plagued the wooden Moscow destroyed many buildings in the Kremlin and in the Metropolitan's estate. After the 1473 fire Metropolitan Geronty had his residence reconstructed; after the 1493 big fire in the Kremlin, Metropolitan Zosima supervised another renovation project. Few records are left of the builders' labors in the Patriarch's estate.

By the late 16th century, the Russian Orthodox Church had been made independent of the Constantinople Patriarch. Instead of the former Metropolitanate, the autonomous Russian Patriarchate was established to be headed by the single leader, the Patriarch of All Russia. On the Moscow Kremlin's plan of the early 17th century, the Patriarch's residence is clearly seen. Roofed passages connected it with the Czar's Terem Palace. Three home churches stood in the Patriarch's estate: the Church of Our Lady's Holy Robe, the Church of Solovetsk Miracle-Workers Zosima and Savvaty, and the Church of the Three Blessed Fathers of Moscow, Peter, Alexei and Jonah.

In July 1652, Novgorod's Metropolitan Nikon was elected Patriarch of Moscow and all Russia. He was Czar Alexei Mikhailovich's choice: the sovereign ruler of Russia believed that only this man of unparalleled will and vigor could become the driving force behind the sweeping church reform begun in the 1640s. With Patriarch Nikon, a new chapter in the history of the Patriarch's Palace was opened. The Czar donated to Nikon a part of former Boris Godunov's estate that

Patriarch Nikon. A miniature from «The Czar's Titlebook». 1672.

was attached to the eastern end of the Patriarch's estate. In September 1652, a new Patriarch's Palace was begun to be erected, and Nikon took active participation in the project. He took great interest primarily in the construction of a new church, the living quarters and the ceremonial Cross Chamber. By the end of 1655, the living, ceremonial and service rooms and the home church had been completed. At that time, the Patriarch's estate was a city in miniature: stone and wooden structures of different purposes, magnificent churches erected and decorated by the nation's best builders and artists.

On the northern end, the huge building completed the ensemble of the Kremlin's Cathedral Square that had been constructed in the 15–16th centuries. Many elements of the Palace's décor were borrowed from the Kremlin's ancient cathedrals: lean «drums» of the five-domed home church resembled those of the Archangel Cathedral; the arcature row on the southern façade was a replica of the Assumption Cathedral's décor. Somewhat sterner is the Patriarch's Palace's northern façade facing the inner yard. The roofed arched gallery on pillars decorated with a row of polychrome tiled shirinkas was attached to the building in the 1690s.

The door whereby the Patriarch entered the Assumption Cathedral.

The Patriarch's new home church was a traditional cruciform-and-domed edifice topped with five cupolas. Arched passageways divided by pilasters supported the building's main

One of the earliest pictures of the Patriarch's Palace. A miniature from «The Book about the Election and Crowning for Reigning of Great Sovereign Czar and Great Prince Mikhail Romanov». 1673.

body. Three drums and two rows of narrow windows allowed much light to the altar and the church's central section. Two more windowless drums stood over of the Patriarch's living quarters.

In the summer of 1656 icon-painters from Russia's famous art centers in Yaroslavl and Kostroma and the St. Sergius-Trinity Monastery led by the talented royal painters Simon Ushakov, Iosif Vladimirov and Feodor Kozlov started to paint the church.

However, «Great Sovereign» Nikon (the Patriarch acquired this new title in 1653 following Patriarch Filaret's example), the Czar's special friend did not rule long. In 1658, he fell out with Alexei Mikhailovich; in 1666, he was defrocked and sent to exile. The home church had long stood non-consecrated. Only in 1680–1, Patriarch Joachim ordered to rebuild the home church erected by the disgraced Nikon. The church was painted anew and consecrated in the name of the Holy Twelve Apostles. According to the old tradition, micaceous plates were inserted in its small windows, the floor was paved with special enameled tiles, and a new carved iconostasis was installed. Art historian assume that for the first time in the history of Russian Orthodoxy the Crucifixion was installed above the upper tier of icons. The new tradition was eventually «instituted everywhere» and marked the Western influence in the Old Russia.

The Patriarch's Palace's northern façade.

The Patriarch's Palace's western wing in the 1640s. A reconstruction by A. Tits.

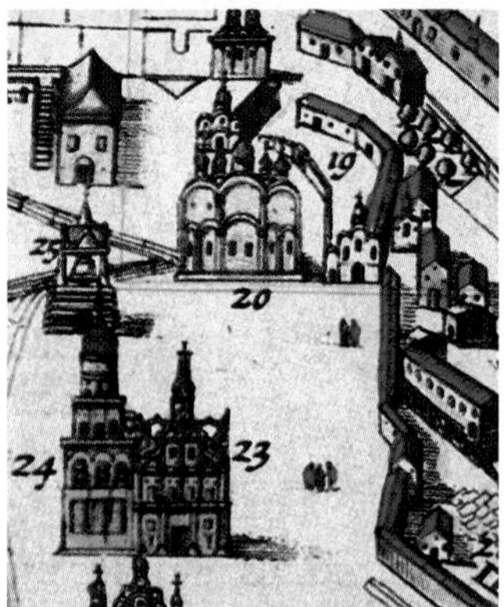

The Godunov Map of the Kremlin, or «the Kremlinagrad». Early 17th century. No. 19 – the Patriarch's Palace.

Thenceforth, the Patriarch's Palace and the Twelve Apostles' Church had been not once rebuilt and refurbished. Thus, in 1722–4, after Peter I abolished the Patriarchate in Russia, the Church was divided by a wooden ceiling into two levels and the Patriarch's library was set up on the upper floor, and a new sacristy in the living quarters. In the mid-19th century, they took away the wooden flooring that divided the Twelve Apostles' Church, and a high wooden iconostasis was installed. Following Czar Nicholas I's order «to give the church

Patriarch Nikon's cowl (above) and sakkos (right). The Moscow Kremlin's workshops. Mid-17th century.

more light», architects widened the old windows and cut the new ones, and changed the outside décor. Under the renovation projects carried out in the 20th century, the original layout of the Patriarch's Palace's rooms on the second and third floors was restored, and the arched passageways under the Twelve Apostles' Church were reopened. In 1929, the iconostasis that had stood in the Ascension Cathedral of the Kremlin's Ascension Monastery was transferred to the Church, together with the marquee-shaped carved canopy from the Chudov Monastery's

Alavaster (vessel for myrrh). Constantinople. Early 17th century.

cathedral. Thus, both masterpieces were saved from inevitable destruction. Under the 1960–70 restoration project, the architectural décor of the eastern façade facing Cathedral Square, service rooms in the Palace's podklet (ground floor), and the original shape of the windows in the first and second stories were restored; and a detail of

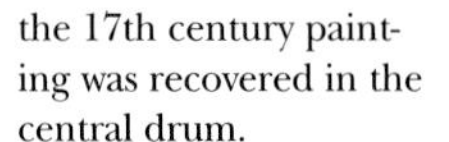

the 17th century painting was recovered in the central drum.

In May of 1987, a permanent exhibition of the Museum of the Russian 17th century Applied Art and Private Life was opened in the second floor. The Palace's third and fourth floors are closed for visitors (a collection of unique fabrics is kept up there). It was based on the main collections of the Moscow Kremlin museums, including the refurbished items of religious and secular applied art that had never before been set to show.

Having ascended the steep stone staircase, you find yourself in the *Maliye Seni* (Lesser Anteroom). Its exposition reconstructs the long history of the Metropolitan's (later, Patriarch's) estate in the Moscow Kremlin. The next room is the Paradniye Seni (Festive Anteroom) where the 17th century religious and secular items that belonged to the Russian Orthodox Church leaders are displayed. Of special interest are patriarch Nikon's ecclesiastical and domestic clothes made of expensive Italian fabrics;

Patriarch Nikon's silver enameled crosier.

A cover for Metropolitan Alexei's coffin. Moscow. The Golden Czarina's Chamber.

the Chudov Monastery – was made in the Kremlin in 1651. Yet another example of outstanding Russian artistic embroidery is a veil «Our Lady of Vladimir» from the sacristy of the Moscow Kremlin's Cathedral of the Assumption. It resembles an icon mounted in a gold frame with inset pearls and precious stones.

The Refectory is connected with the Twelve Apostles' Church that houses one of the most interesting displays of the exhibition. The

Holy-water bowl. The Moscow Kremlin's workshops. 1625.

Left: Oversleeves with pearl embroidery. 17th century.

headwear – patriarch Filaret's and Nikon's hoods; Filaret's, Nikon's and Adrian's carved and chased crosiers, as well as numerous silverware the Patriarchs normally used.

Leaving the Festive Anteroom, you can turn left and go into the eastern wing. You are in the Refectory. Here, you can see a unique collection of Old Russian figurative and ornamental embroidery displayed in the showcases. The collection deserves your attention! This special kind of applied art – mainly, only women commanded enough skill – was known in Old Russia everywhere. The skill required special training and patience, too, as it took sometimes years to complete just one article. The typical feature of the 17th century figurative embroidery is the predominance of gold threads, precious metals and stones, and pearls over soft polychromatic silk. The Metropolitan Alexei's coffin cloth – Czar Alexei Mikhailovich's and Czarina Maria Iliyinichna's donation to

Icon «Our Lady with Acathistus». Detail. Mid-17th century.

magnificent five-tiered iconostasis made of carved gilded wood in the Russian baroque manner, is the first to draw your attention. It strikes an onlooker by a diversity of its ornamental motifs and its plastic vividness. Its vegetation patterns include flowers, leaves, fruits, berries, heavy grapes. The iconostasis' architectural design – a protruding cornice, twisted columns, pilasters, and an arch over the king's gate – is expressive and diverse. This type of intricate carving was in harmony with the new tendencies in Russian icon painting of that time – namely, reproducing space in perspective and accurate rendering of three-dimensional figures.

At present, the Twelve Apostles' Church houses a rich collection of the 17th century Russian icons, most of which once belonged to the Kremlin's cathedrals and monasteries. The earliest ones hang on the southern wall. They represent the key trend of the early 17th century Russian icon painting, the so-called «Stroganoff» school. The name is arbitrary, though, and is related to the clan of the wealthy Moscow merchants and philanthropists. The icons «The Lord Rested on the Seventh Day» and «In the Coffin of Flesh» are small-sized yet multifigurative, bright, polychromatic, meticulously painted and lavishly gilded. The artistic principles of «the Stroganoff School» defined the tendencies in icon painting

The Twelve Apostles' Church's iconostasis. 1680s.

Painting on the lower tier of the over-the-throne marquee-shaped canopy. Moscow. 1641.

up to the mid-17th century. The fine art of «the Stroganoff school» is embodied in the icon «Praise of Our Lady with Acathistus», that may have been painted by Yaroslavl's icon-painters. In the middle section, Mary wearing a royal robe and a crown sits with Christ in her lap on a beautiful see, surrounded by 16 prophets depicted in oval medallions made of green stems and bright flowers. The composition is framed by 24 margins of the Acathistus, a religious hymn dedicated to Our Lady, with inscriptions on the borders.

In the icons made in the second half of 17th century, the Old Russian tradition of painting is dropped in favor of a new «realistic» trend. The new artistic principles found the most vivid expression in the art of the «certified» icon-painters of the Armory Chamber, Simon Ushakov, Fedor Zubov, Kirill Ulanov, Ivan Saltanov and others. Such is, for instance, «Theodore Stratilat» by Simon Ushakov from the Archangels' Cathedral. The saint is standing and praying, wearing the colorful garment. His face is rendered in three-dimensional manner, graphically and expressively; while seeking full «life-likeness», the painter meticulously depicted the shape of the saint's eyes and even the eyelashes.

After Simon Ushakov died, Feodor Zubov was invited from Velikiy Ustyug to Moscow and appointed head of the court painters. His icon «Andrei, the First Summoned» from the Kremlin's Chudov Monastery is remarkable in its psychological depth. The apostle is painted full-length, with a scroll in his left hand; he gives a blessing with his right hand. The saint's

«Savior on the Throne». The iconostasis' local tier. Moscow. 1680s.

Icon «John the Warrior». Moscow. Late 17th century.

Right: «Andrei the First Summoned». Feodor Zubov. 1669.

face gives a stunning impression: it is both woeful and spirited. Just take a look at a background landscape in the late 17th century icon «Jonah the Warrior», and at architectural and landscape backdrops in Fyodor Nikitin-Rozhnov's icon «Crucifixion with the Apostles' Passions» from the Cathedral of the Assumption that was painted upon Patriarch Adrian's order. Of special interest is Kirill Ulanov's «Our Lady's Nativity» painted in 1699 for the Assumption Cathedral's Pokhvalskiy Chapel.

Interior of a living room with the authentic pieces of medieval furniture from an affluent Russian home.

Chair. Moscow. 17th century. Restored in 1980s.

Tiled stove on the Patriarch's Palace's second floor. Early 18th century.

Having visited the Church, you can go to the living quarters (after you return to the Refectory, turn right). The two rooms appear in their original architectural design, whereas the exposition here helps imagine the typical way of life of Old Muscovy's rich people. Among the curious items of the 17th century are the celestial globe, a set of chess, a pair of spectacles, a micaceous lantern. Old printed and hand-written books give a vivid impression of the art of book publishing and the level of public education in the late 17th century Russia. Most interesting are Melety Smotritsky's printed grammar book published in 1647 and Karion Izmailov's handwritten ABC of 1693. The ABC was written in black ink and illuminated in watercolor with gilding. The author, Moscow Printing Office's printer and the then famous poet and writer, gave this hand-

Micaceous lantern. 17th century.

The marble myrrh-making oven under the gilded canopy in the Cross Chamber. 1763.

The 200-kg silver myrrh-container. A gift of Empress Katherine II. 1767.

written copy of his ABC to the son of Peter the Great, Alexei. The book was published by the Court's Printing Office in two printings (engraver Leoniy Bunin).

The Patriarch's Palace's ceremonial hall is the Cross Chamber. The Chamber's design was regarded as a novelty in the mid-17th century and reflected the high level of craftsmanship of Russian stone builders. A huge hall of 280 sq. meters was covered by a high vault without a central pillar. Solid walls (over 2 meters thick), reinforced on both sides by iron links, carried the burden of the arch. Large windows with deep- cut and wide-sloped frames emphasized the splendor of the ceremonial chamber, and enhanced an impression of its interior's magnificence.

Abraamiy Palitsin announces in the Cross Chamber that the first Romanov was just elected Czar. A miniature from «The Book about the Election and Crowning for Reigning of Great Sovereign Czar and great Prince Mikhail Romanov». 1672–1673.

The Cross Chamber was devised to be the Patriarch's chapel, where the higher clergy gathered on special holidays: the white clergy (Metropolitans in white hoods) and the black clergy (archbishops and bishops in black hoods). Besides, sessions attended by the higher clergy and the Patriarch were held here to decide on the key ecclesiastical issues. Church Councils were regularly held in the Cross Chamber, too.

In 1763, a large stove for making the church oil, myrrh, was installed in the Cross Chamber, and since then, this room was often called the Myrrh-making Chamber. In the late 18th century, the Chamber was renovated according to Matvei Kazakov's design.

The Cross Chamber houses the Museum's largest collection of items made mainly by Moscow's and the Kremlin's masters. A great variety of copper and tin articles were made by town craftsmen, whereas the craftsmen employed in the Kremlin's royal and patriarchal workshops made articles decorated with precious and semi-precious stones and pearls. A showcase opposite the entrance reconstructs the Old Russian pyramidal postavets. Such tables were used as an eye-catching decorative item in Old Russian ceremonial banquet rooms.

The Cross Chamber's exhibit.

Clock «Turk on Horseback». Augusburg. 17th century.

Tower clock. The Netherlands. Late 17th century.

The rich collection of Old Russian tableware represents the fine and sophisticated techniques of gold- and silversmiths. It features different-sized plates and dishes, bowls and goblets, tall cups and small dippers, as well as large ladles and loving cups still widely used in the 17th century. Among the many examples of Old Russian embossment, a frame for the icon of Our Lady is the gem of the collection. It is a masterpiece of the early 17th century jewelry, with an elegant stylized pattern and finely selected jewels in beautiful mounts.

Embossed items – plates, glasses, frames of the polychromatic enameled items made by enamellists in the town of Solvychegodsk in the southern part of the Archangelsk region.

Goblet with a lid. Nuremberg. Second half of the16th century.

Ladle made of birchwood. 17th century.

Amulet stand (a tree for amulets). Moscow. First half of the 17th century.

Bowl. Solvychegodsk. Second half of the 17th century.

Right: Salt-cellar. Moscow. Late 17th century.

Silver buttons. 17th century.

gospels – were often decorated with niello and enamel. After a long period of neglect, enameling was again on the rise in Russia in late 16th–17th centuries as a leading decorative technique used in jeweler's art. Over centuries, pattern-making methods, as well as patterns and colors changed, but the very technique of enameling always required much skill and experience. Of special interest are

Jewelry and dress paraphernalia of the Old Russian stylish women represents the Old Russian jewelers' art. The portrait of Czar Peter the Great's aide Peter Ivanovich Potemkin who headed the Russian mission to France and Spain in 1684 renders all the splendor and grandeur of a Russian ceremonial costume (you could see it hanging in one of the Palace's living rooms). In the olden times, claspers, buckles, buttons, besides being useful little things, were worn as decorative articles accentuating the splendor and luxury of a men's or women's dress. Do pay attention to the splendid collection of enameled golden and silver buttons with inset precious stones. Such buttons were the special mark of an Old Russian vestment. According to the fashion or the technique used in the 16–17th century, buttons differed as «pear-shaped», «acorn-shaped», half-shaped, carved, sprinkled-on, plain...

In the 16th and especially 17th century, many items made by West European masters were brought to Russia, mainly silverware: goblets for expensive Rhine wines, cups, containers for dry goods, sugared fruits and pickles. Following the instructions of their Russian clients, craftsmen in Hamburg, Augusburg and Nuremberg sometimes made the tableware in traditional Russian style – for instance, bratina loving cups and ladles. Foreign-made domestic items – weapons, fabrics and jewelry – were also in great demand.

Gospel. Moscow printing house. 1681. Book-holder. Moscow. 1685.

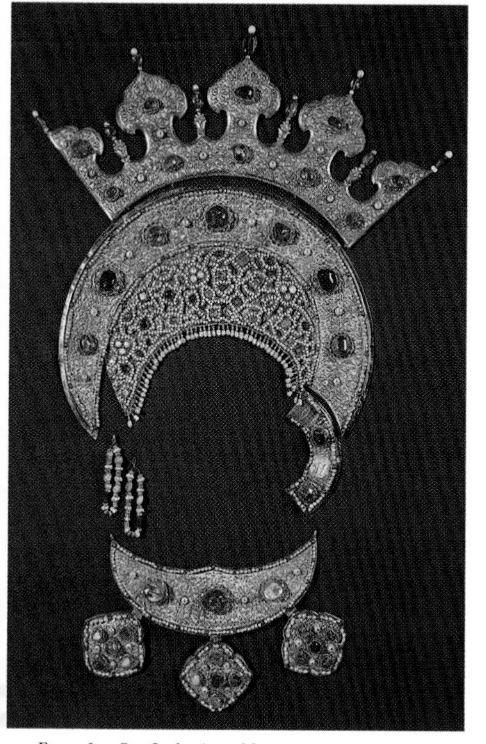

Frame for «Our Lady» icon. Moscow. Late 16th–early 17th century.

Quite remarkable is the collection of old watches and clocks. Table clocks were used as decoration of the ceremonial chambers. Wristwatches worn on long chains were set to show as an expensive toy. At that time, watches and clocks were brought to Russia from Germany, England and France, but foreign clockmakers did work in the Kremlin, too. The copper gilded book-watch with chased images reportedly belonged to Ivan the Terrible. The golden powder-flask watch decorated with niello and chased ornaments belonged to Czar Alexei Mikhailovich.

A FAREWELL TO THE KREMLIN

Each era in the Russian history sought to leave its lasting imprint in the Moscow Kremlin. Many edifices built in later years organically fit into the magnificent architectural ensemble.

The Senate, a superb example of the Russian classicism.

Leaving the Patriarch's Palace you will see in front of you a three-story building – the Senate, the true masterpiece of the Russian 18th century classicism. It was built in 1776–78, according to the design of the outstanding architect Matvei Kazakov, on the site where the estates of boyars Trubetskoy and Bortnyansky once were located. Initially, the building was devised for the regular sessions of Moscow's nobility representatives. In 1856, however, it was given over to the Moscow City Senate.

The building, if seen from above, is shaped as a triangle with cut angles and has an inner yard divided by passages into three sections. In the middle of the main façade, there is an arched passage leading into the inner yard. This passage is fashioned like a triumphal arch with a four-column portico and a fronton. Inside the majestic rotund topped with a gigantic green cupola the Yekateriniskiy (Catherine's) Hall is located. The Hall's diameter is 25 m; its height is 27 m. It is adorned along its perimeter by the Corinthian columns and high reliefs showing Russian Prince sand Czars. These are plaster copies of the marble originals made by Fedor Shubin in 1785 for the Chesmenskiy Palace in St. Petersburg (now kept in the Armory Chamber). Allegorical low-relief figures over the doors represent Enlightenment, Justice, Law and Virtue. Ascetic white-blue decoration of the walls goes in harmony with the snow-white columns and the furniture's blue upholstery. The imposing Yekaterininskiy hall was nicknamed «the Russian pantheon» by the contemporaries.

The Senate's inner yard.

The green cupola and the blowing Russian tri-colored flag are well seen from Red Square. Once, the cupola was topped with the statue of St. George the Victor. The retreating French soldiers destroyed it in 1812. After 1856, the cupola was adorned with a pole and an inscription «Law». After the 1917 revolution, the Senate building housed the Kremlin workers and army cadets' club. A year later, when the Russian capital was moved from St. Petersburg down to Moscow, the Senate came to be the Russian (later Soviet) government's home. A red flag was fixed over its cupola. In this building, the first Soviet leader Vladimir Lenin lived; subsequently, Josef Stalin worked in here. These days, this building

The Arsenal's eastern façade and the Nikolskaya Tower.

The cannons at the Arsenal's southern façade.

is the official residence of the President of the Russian Federation and it houses the President's Office.

On the left of the Senate, you can see the Arsenal, or, as they used to say in older days, «The Armory House». It was begun to be built in 1702, upon Czar Peter I's order as an armaments and ammunition storehouse. In 1706, because of the war with Sweden, the construction works were suspended and resumed only in 1722 to be completed 14 years later. The year of the construction project's completion – 1736 – is carved on the gate's frame. But the next year the Arsenal was burned down. In 1786–96, the building was restored by an engineer W. Gerard under the supervision of Matvei Kazakov. In 1812, prior to their retreat from Moscow, the French invaders blew a portion of Arsenal. 16 years later it was restored and then preserved until today. The trapeze-shaped low edifice with a sizable inner yard and two arched passageways is made of brick. Its walls are adorned with sculpted images of military items. The double windows, with snow-white oval platbands, rhythmically repeated along the façade give an impression of solid durability.

A Russian cannon.

The building's height is 24 m.

A special 18th century decree instructed to collect foreign made weaponry and Russian cannons in the Arsenal. After 1812, it was transformed into the Patriotic War museum. 875 French cannons were added to the old collection. The Russian and foreign cannons installed along the Arsenal's southeastern façade is a sort of an open-air extra to the Armory Chamber's collection. Of special interest are 20 Russian cannons made in the 16–17th century by famous Russian casters. Among them are «The Troilus» by Andrei Chokhov (1590), «The Wolf» by Jakov Dubina (1659), «The Gamayun» by Martyn Osipov (1690). The foreign cannons were cast in Paris, Lyon, Breslau and other

A memorial plate fixed near the Arsenal in commemoration of the Kremlin garrison's soldiers killed in combat while defending Moscow and the Kremlin's airspace from Nazi bombers during the 1941–45 Great Patriotic War.

The former Presidium of the Supreme Soviet Building.

European cities in the late 18 – early 19th century.

On the Arsenal's southern façade, near the arch, two memorial plates are fixed: the one, in commemoration of the Red Guard soldiers shot by the Yunkers on October 28 of 1917, the other, in the memory of the Kremlin garrison's soldiers killed in combat while defending Moscow and the Kremlin's airspace from Nazi bombers during the 1941–45 Great Patriotic War.

The Lion cannon. Master Karp Balasheich. 1705.

During the 20th century, many cathedrals and monasteries were dismantled in the Kremlin. On the vacant lots, numerous new buildings were erected. One of them is the administrative building constructed in 1932–34 near the Spasskaya Tower (designed by Ilya

Rherberg). Initially, it was devised for the Red Commanding Officers School. Later it housed the Kremlin's Theatre, and then the Presidium of the USSR Supreme Council (the main legislative body of the Soviet Union). The architect managed to organically incorporate the new building into the ensemble of the Kremlin's palatial edifices, as he made it reflect the shape and coloring of the adjacent Senate's classical façade. Its interior was drastically changed in the 1960s. At present, the building houses various departments of the Russian President's Office, the Kremlin Commandant's Office and other administrative agencies.

From its Festive Vestibule, the two side staircases lead to the Main Lobby on the second floor. Here, an enfilade of parade halls is located; the hall's interior decor repeats the Kremlin's old palatial rooms. Rare kinds of decorative minerals and wood, precious fabrics, unique furniture and lamps give the enfilade's interiors special look. The enfilade begins with the Avanzal (Anteroom), a small square-shaped room with the mirror wall that visually enlarges its dimensions. Adjacent to it is the Reception Hall where foreign ambassadors hand over to the Presidents their credentials. The last is the Meeting Room whose interior is decorated in light colors (you may have seen it in TV reports from the Kremlin).

The Kremlin's State Palace.

A passage between the Kremlin's State Palace and the Patriarch's Palace.

Another 20th century structure in the ancient Kremlin is the huge box of glass and white marble. It is the Kremlin's State Palace (earlier, the Kremlin's Palace of Congresses).

The Alexandrov Gardens. The yellow building of the Arsenal can be seen behind the Kremlin's wall.

Walking from the Patriarch's Palace to the Troitskaya Tower you can see it on your left. The State Palace is connected with the Patriarch's Palace by a passage.

The State Palace was built in 1959–61 for the congresses of the then ruling Communist Party of the Soviet Union. It is still the biggest public building in Moscow; there are 800 rooms of different size and purpose, including the enormous 6,000-seat conference hall with the world's largest stage. In the 1980–early 1990s, major state and international events were held in this hall: sessions of the USSR Supreme Soviet, congresses of the People's Deputies, and international forums.

In recent years, the Palace's main conference hall has been mainly used as a concert hall to stage ballet performances, entertainment shows. The prestigious and often televised «concerts in the Kremlin» by Russian and international pop stars (Philip Kirkorov, Elton John, Tina Turner, Eric Clapton and so forth) are held in the Kremlin's State Palace.

A peculiar ancient edifice with a marquee-shaped roof – the Fun Palace – is almost hidden in between the Kremlin's State Palace and the Kremlin's wall. Unfortunately, you cannot come closer to it, as these days it houses the Kremlin Commandant's Office. However, you can take a look at it standing near the corner of the Kremlin's Large Palace.

A fountain of the Manezhnaya Square shopping mall. Sculptor Zurab Tsereteli.

In 1651 boyar Ivan Miloslavskiy, the father of Czar Alexei Mikhailovich's first wife, built a three-story stone house for himself. After he died in 1668, his residence was commandeered by the treasury.

Then the former Miloslavskiy's house was a little remodeled in order to stage «fun parties» – special histrionic performances for the Czar, the Czar's family

The Alexandrov Gardens in summer. In the background, the yellow building of Manezh is seen.

The Fun Palace as seen from the Lion's Gate. A watercolor by F. Solntsev. First half of the 19th century.

and the court. In 1679, upon Czar Feodor Alexeyevich's order, the Fun Palace was given over to the czarevnas as their living quarters.

The parade entrance was located on the southern façade with the Lion's Gate, a remarkable architectural masterwork. On the third floor, a home church and a small belfry on four pylons were built. The Fun Palace's residents could go across the street, via the wooden passages propped on poles, to the Terem Palace.

In the late 18th century, the Fun Palace was reconstructed under the supervision of I. Yegotov. The next major renovation took place in the Palace in the second half of the 19th century. Architect N. Shokhin tried to restore the 17th century original layout and the outside décor. He built a new white-stone portal on the eastern façade, whose columns were decorated with melon-shaped links and covered with filigree ornamental carving. Of the greatest esthetic value are the few preserved parts of the original building (the white-stone portals, the platbands) facing the Kremlin's wall. These remains allowed the art historians to conclude that in its time, the Fun Palace was a remarkable item of the Old Russian architecture.

Well, you have approached the Troitskiye Gate leading to the Kutafiya Tower over the Troitskiy Bridge. From the Bridge you can admire the wonderful panorama of the Alexandrov Gardens.

The Fun Palace as seen from its inner yard. A 19th century drawing.

THE KREMLIN'S TREASURES

«What can be compared to this Kremlin, which, surrounded by merloned walls, featuring golden domes of its cathedrals, lays on a high hill like a stately crown on the awesome ruler's head...» Thus wrote in the 1830 a young officer Mikhail Lermontov. Several years later, yet another gem was to be added to this crown, the Kremlin's Large Palace gloriously standing on the edge of the Borovitskiy Hill. For many decades, only those privileged few had the rare right to admire its superlative interiors. Since 1955, the Moscow Kremlin's visitors were allowed to get acquainted with the Palace's treasures.

The Kremlin's Large Palace.

The cast-iron fence between the Armory Chamber and the Kremlin's Large Palace.

To the left of the Kremlin's Large Palace, near the Borovitskiye Gate, stands a two-story long edifice that houses one the nation's oldest museums, the Armory Chamber. The best masterpieces of the Russian and foreign decorative and applied art are displayed in its spacious halls. No museum around the world can possibly boast of having the comparable collections as those of ancient fabrics or German silverwork.

Tickets to the Armory Chamber can be bought either at the Kremlin's ticket-office in the Alexandrov Gardens or in the Chamber itself. However, you should better buy the tickets days in advance. Visitors are admitted to the museum in shifts (one séance lasts for 1 hour 15 minutes), so tickets may be sold out. The Kremlin's Large Palace and the Diamond Fund exhibition may be visited according to a special schedule. Ask them at the Excursion Office to help you with getting the tickets.

Left: the parade doors of the Kremlin's Large Palace's Alexandrovskiy Hall.

THE ARMORY CHAMBER

The precious items from the personal treasury that were supposed to be passed on to heirs, were mentioned in Great Princes' last wills back in the 14th century. In the 15th century, the Treasury Court to store the Great Prince's coffers was constructed near the Archangel's and Annunciation Cathedrals. It was then considered a state treasury rather than a personal one. The items kept in the Treasury Court were used during coronation ceremonies, official receptions, special church services.

For the first time, the Armory Chamber was mentioned in 1547. It was a sort of a workshop where regal weaponry and armor were made. At the same time, a number of separate workshops for making regular household items sprang up in the late 16th–17th century: they were called the Silver, the Gold and the Czarina's Chambers. Subsequently, they were incorporated into the Armory Chamber, or Armory Department. The nation's best craftsmen as well as foreign masters invited to Russia worked there. In 1640, an icon-making workshop was established, and in 1683, a painting workshop.

Both the Armory Chamber and the Kremlin's other workshops had come to be the center of Russian art and handicraft that boomed and flourished in the second half of the 17th century. When in the early 18th century, the royal court moved up to St. Petersburg, some of the Kremlin's craftsmen followed their regal principals. So, the Armory Chamber was transformed into a warehouse of ancient treasures. In 1806, its collection helped create a public museum; and in 1806–1810, a special building (designed by I. Yegotov) was erected opposite the Arsenal to house the museum. The national treasures had been kept in the old Armory Chamber building up to the mid-19th century. The present0-day building was created by Konstantin Ton in 1851. Its parade façade facing the Moskva River is painted yellow and decorated with carved white stone elements in the 17th century manner.

The museum consists of nine halls: four on the ground floor and five on the first floor. It would not be an exaggeration to say that each of 4,000 items on display here is unique in itself and deserves a special lecture. It is simply impossible to describe in a small

The Armory Chamber's parade staircase. Architect Konstantin Ton.

Icon «Dmitry Solunskiy». Byzantium. 11th–14th century.

Ark. Russia. Suzdal. 1383.

Gospel. Moscow. 1499.

booklet the museum's exhibition in its entirety – and no one would ask for it. You may want to fully rely on the guided excursions led by well-qualified specialists who will be happy to show you the most interesting exhibits and answer any question. Or, you can borrow an audio-player with a prerecorded explanation and browse through the exposition on your own.

A small collection of Byzantine artworks

Barmas (Russian princes' shoulder decorations) from the Ryazan trove. The pieces are 7.5 cm to 12.5 cm in diameter.

consists of jewelry pieces, cameos, silver plate and religious items of the 5th–15th century. The collection of cameos dating back to the 11th– 12th century shows images of Christian saints carved in stone (agate, lapis, jasper, steatite). Of special interest are the works by Byzantine goldsmiths and silversmiths, chasers and enamellists. The art of enameling came to this country from Byzantium, as Old Russia had maintained diplomatic and trade relations with it since the 10th century.

A sizeable collection of jewelry embracing the 12th – early 20th century period introduces you to the history of Russian jewelers' art. Just take a look at the so called Ryazan trove found in 1822 and dated back to the 12th century. In addition to women's precious toys, there are magnificently enameled and filigreed regal insignia and religious items, like a Great Prince's shoulder decorations (barmas) with pearls and precious stones and a golden holy-relic holder showing the composition «The Descent into Hell».

The incense-burner from the Archangels' Cathedral. The Moscow Kremlin's workshops. 1598. Czarina Irina Godunova's gift.

Gospel. The Moscow Kremlin's workshops. 1571.

The Novgorod exhibit includes tiny icons, crosses and panagias, church plate and household items, like, for instance, Novgorod Archbishop Moisey's church goblet made of jasper and the 15th century ladles. The silver ark that was specially made to keep the holy relics brought by archbishop Dionysy from Constantinople in the 14th century, is considered a true masterpiece of Suzdal silversmiths. Very interesting are the pieces done by Moscow jewelers of the 14th–15th century: silver and golden icon- and book- frames, church plate – especially gilded arks (the Bigger and Lesser zions) made, upon the request of Great Prince Ivan III, for the Assumption Cathedral.

The 16th century was hailed as the golden era – both literally and figuratively – of the Russian applied art. In 1547, Great Prince «of all Russia» Ivan IV was crowned for czardom. The newly crowned Czar's public appearances and reception parties were orchestrated with ever more magnificence and splendor. The Kremlin's masters' style was characterized by sophisticated plainness and the elegance of the clear and austere ornamentation. They tended to adorn crosses, icons, Gospels and secular pieces with complicated filigree ornaments sometimes painting them in transparent enamel.

Silverware was in vogue then. Golden plates were rarely used and were rather gift items lavishly covered with chased and niello ornaments. Just take notice of the superb golden dish with a fine velvety niello brim – what a striking example of stylish and elegant craftsmanship! This is a wedding gift by Czar Ivan the Terrible to his second wife, Kabarda Princess Maria Temryukovna. Among the masterpieces of the period, pay your attention to the golden frame on the 1571 Gospel book donated by Ivan the Terrible to the Annunciation Cathedral, and to the three sardonix cameos showing Virgin Mary, John the Ladder-builder and John the Precursor. Of special artistic value are the golden goblet and a incense-burner, the gift of Czar Feodor ioannovich's wife Czarina Irina Godunova to the Moscow Kremlin's Archangel's Cathedral. Both were made in the Kremlin's workshops in 1598. Since the early 17th century, upon the patriarch's instruction, this burner was allowed to be used only on major church holidays, nine times a year.

Unforgettable are finely wrought-out silver chased lids for the tombs of Czarevich Dmitry and Kirill Belozerskiy made in the Kremlin's Silversmith's Chamberin the first half of the 17th century. The new century's goldsmiths and craftsmen, while meticulously following the manner of their predecessors used also new techniques: enamel on high relief embossment, decorative enamel-painting, fine niello.

In the 17th century, the Kremlin's craftsmen and artists were strictly separated by profession: filigree-masters, chasers, enamellists, niello-makers etc. The palatial ceremonies, as well as the Czars' lavish everyday life in the mid-17th century, required that a huge variety of diverse items, both secular and religious, were used. According to the survived archival documents and inventories, the Russian golden and silver tableware aroused great interest among foreign guests. The Armory Chamber houses the world's largest collection of such tableware, including ladles and bratina loving cups, dippers and cups, bowls and dishes.

A ball-shaped bratina covered with complicated chased ornament and a chased inscription along its rim, is a unique example of the then typical tableware. The bratina, a ball-shaped bowl on a short thick stem, sometimes with a cone-shaped lid, was used for «celebration drinking» when the filled bowl was handed over down the line of guests. Also, there were personal bratinas, for both men and women. An example of the latter is the small golden bratina that belonged to Czar Mikhail Feodorovich's wife Czarina Evdokia Lukyanovna. You can see in this collection an absolutely exceptional piece of Russian silverware, yendova. The purpose of this round vessel with a beak is not known – perhaps, it contained strong alcoholic drinks available on the table. Usually, strong drinks were served in korchiks, small ladles on a tray, and charkas. They were made of crystal, carved

Church Goblet. Bowl – Novgorod. Early 16th century. Base – France. 14th century.

Ladle. The Moscow Kremlin's workshops. 1618. Belonged to Czar Mikhail Feodorovich.

Yendova. Moscow. 1644. Belonged to boyar V. Streshnev.

of bone or semi-precious stones, inserted into golden or silver holders with chased inscriptions along the rim referring to the piece's owner.

The works of Russian jewelers of the second half of the 17th century will impress you with the elegance and lavishness of décor, the richness and clarity of enamel colors, with the radiance of the precious stones. The true gem of the exhibit is the golden bowl given in 1653 by Patriarch Nikon to Czar Alexei Mikhailovich, and the golden goblet featuring bright enameled ornamentation that was donated by boarynya Morozova to the Kremlin's Chudov monastery in 1664. Of special interest is the 1678 Gospel in gold frame with enamel ornament and precious stones. The frame was made upon Czar Feodor Mikhailovich's order for the Kremlin's palatial home Church of Veronica.

At the time, emeralds were much loved and widely used by Russian jewelers. Thus, the frame of the «Our Lady of Vladimir» icon that was made in 1657 on Patriarch Nikon's instruction, is decorated by two gigantic emeralds, 100 carats each. The so called «flower style» was gradually coming into fashion then: the images of flowers, mostly tulips, abounded in carved and niello ornaments.

In the 17th–early 18th century, local jewelry schools were gaining more success and fame. So, the Moscow Kremlin invited craftsmen from Yaroslavl, Kostroma, Nizhniy Novgorod, Solvychegodsk. Their art is represented in the Armory Chamber exhibit, too. Beginning in the late 18th century, the jeweler's art was on the boom in Russian cities, and many pieces were made of decorative rather than practical purpose.

Gospel. The Moscow Kremlin's workshops. 1678. Czar Feodor Alexeyevich's gift to the Kremlin's Verkhospasskiy Cathedral.

Plate. The Moscow Kremlin's workshops. 1618–1676. Belonged to boyar B. Khitrovo.

Frame of the icon «Our Lady of Vladimir». The Moscow Kremlin's workshops. 1657. Master P. Ivanov.

«Dandelion».
St. Petersburg.
Karl Faberge workshop.
1914–1917.

Siberian city of Tobolsk in 1779.

The articles created in the famous Karl Faberge workshop are looming large in the 19th–early 20th century jewelry collection. For his workshop, Karl Faberge had pulled together a team of the best jewelers and artists – all in all, about 500 men worked under him. His jewelers made tobacco-boxes, powder-boxes, broaches, rings, spectacles. The Faberge trademark, though, were Easter surprise-eggs with tiniest silver and golden pieces set inside (like, for instance, a miniature model of the «Pamyat' Azova» cruiser or a golden miniature train inside the Trans-Siberian Railway egg). The Faberge workshop was famous for its transparent and thick enamels (featuring up to 500 shades of color) and was the first in Russia to make use of crystal jasper, heliotrope, onyx etc. The Faberge masters utilized utterly unusual materials. Thus, in «Dandelion» they used the real flower's down. After 85 years, the specially treated dandelion's down has preserved its freshness and liveliness.

Surprise egg with a miniature model of the Emperor's yacht «Standart». Karl Faberge's workshop. 1914–1917.

«Turtle» box. St. Petersburg. Karl Faberge workshop. 1914–1917.

Thus, for example, is the cooking pan made by the Vologda-based jeweler S. Skripitsyn in 1837 or a silver plate made in Moscow in 1814 and given to count M. Platov, a hero of the Borodino Battle, or a tea set made in the

Arm-armor. Turkey. Late 16th – early 17th century.

Dagger. Blade – Iran. First half of the 16th century. Handle and scabbard – Turkey. 17th century.

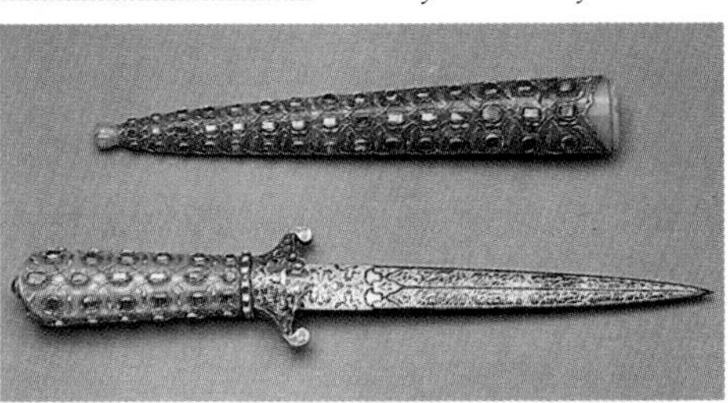

The Russian weapons of the 12th–early 19th century are on display in the so-called Round Hall. You can get there via the filigree iron gate with the Russian Empire state emblem in the center and Russian cities' coats of arms on its sides. By the time the Kremlin's Armory Chamber was first mentioned in the chronicle, it had housed a sizeable set of arms and armor. Back in 1511, Great Prince Vassiliy Ivanovich introduced the rank of armory-man who was obliged to watch for the Prince's arms. In the 16th–17th century the collection was supplemented by parade and hunting pieces made in the Kremlin's workshops. Later, the battle trophies and Old Russian weapons and ammunition were kept in the Armory Chamber. Thus, you can see a late 12th-early 13th century helmet that might have belonged to Prince Yaroslav Vsevolodovich, the father of Alexander Nevskiy. *Kolchuga* (chain armor) was a key element of a Rus-

Shield. Iran. 16th century.

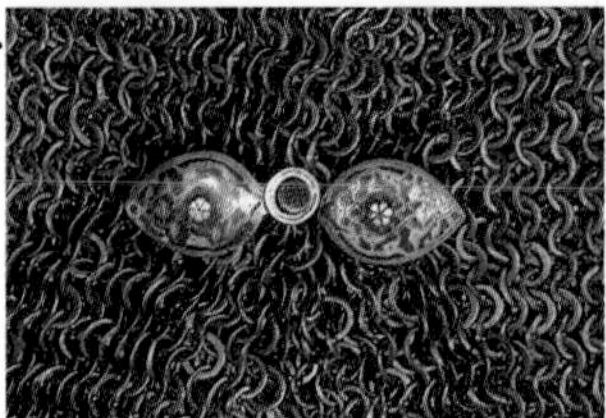

Chain armor. Russia. Late 16th century. Belonged to Czar Boris Godunov.

Below: chain armor's weave-work. Detail.

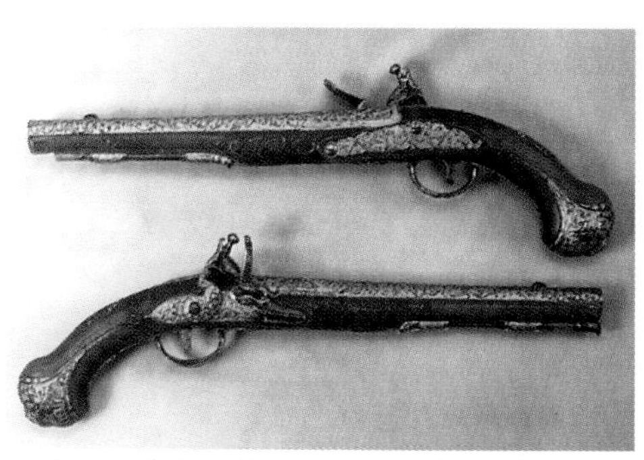

Pistols. Moscow. First quarter of the 17th century. Master Pervusha Isayev.

Saber and scabbard. Zlatoust. 1729 Master Ivan Bushuyev.

sian warrior's equipment. Just imagine how hard it was to fight in a battlefield wearing a 16-kg kolchuga made of thousands of iron rings. Over the kolchuga, the warriors would often put on a «zertsalo» (mirror), well-polished metal plates.

The most used type of weaponry in the 16th–17th century were

Helmet with mask. Early 16th century.

swords, sabers, and knives with solid steel blades and bone handles. However, in the last 14th century, firearms appeared in Russia. In the 15th century, the Cannon Court, where cannon were made, was established in Moscow. The large part of the museum's collection are parade and hunting guns and pistols made in the Kremlin, in Tula, Sestroretsk, Zlatoust and other Russian centers of firearm-making. Also, on display are the 15th–early 19th century firearms and armor made in England, Holland, Germany, Italy. As a rule, a set of armor weighed 30 kg and it was only possible to wage a fight when on horseback. The Armory Chamber collection features the unique parade armor set for a warrior and a horse created in Nuremberg in 1584 and given to Czar Feodor Ivanovich by Polish King Stephan Batory.

Czar Alexei Mikhailovich's zertsalo.Master Nikita Davydov.

A special part of the collection are the 16th–17th century pieces of arms from Iran and Turkey that were added to the treasury from ambassadorial gifts and purchases abroad. Just look at the shield made by Iranian craftsmen that belonged to Prince Feodor Mstislavskiy. Due to its unparalleled artistic value it was included in the Armory Chamber's 1687 inventory as entry No. 1.

Steel ax. Iran. 17th century.

Eagle. Germany, Augusburg. 17th century. Masters A. Drentwett, H. Mannlich.

Helmet. Turkey. Late 16th – early 17th century.

The most interesting part of the exhibit are the ambassadorial and diplomatic gifts from Western Europe, especially silver and golden tableware: dishes, goblets, bowls etc. The vast collection of West European silver includes jewelry pieces from Augusburg, Hamburg, Nuremberg, Paris. In addition, you can see magnificent sets, including «The Olympic» painted porcelain set made in Sevres – the gift of Napoleon to Emperor Alexander I in commemoration of the 1807 Tilsit peace treaty. The set consists of 140 items, and no painted images on either of them are repeated.

A unique collection of rare fabrics – Russian European and Oriental – is yet another treasure of the Armory Chamber's exhibit. Foreign made fabrics were often used for making parade garments of the Russian Czars and Patriarchs. Most valued were Byzantine satins used for the higher clergy's robes. Such fabrics are displayed, besides the Kremlin's Armory Chamber, in only London and Athens.

Of special interest is a collection of the 16th–17th century clothes. The earliest exhibit is Metropolitan Philipp's fur-coat he wore while in exile in the Otoroch Monastery in Tver to the north of Moscow. Besides, you can see kaftans of different fashions and purposes, including the one that belonged to Czar Peter I. The over-armor (it was put on over the parade armor) is a single example of this kind of Old Russian dress.

In early 186th century Peter I issued a decree whereby he substituted the modern European clothes for the traditional Old Russian garb. The coronation dress of Peter's wife, Empress Katherine I, was made according to the newly introduced European fashion. Empress Elisabeth Petrovna's coronation dress is exceptionally splendid, as only her mantle weighed 5 kg. Generally speaking, Elisabeth Petrovna was far from indifferent to clothes: her wardrobe contained 15,000 pieces of dresses.

Invaluable is the collection of the Russian decorative embroidery – palls, kerchiefs, napkins and the like items of the household and religious use. Embroideresses created the stunning works of art that in expressiveness could only be matched to magnificent icons and frescoes. Russian female artists were famous for their ability to cope with pearls. The cover for a priest's robe made in the Kremlin's Czarina's Chamber, Czar Mikhail Feodorovich's gift to the Novospasskiy Monastery, is widely considered as the best example of decorative embroidery. You may inspect for hours these finely wrought pieces appreciative of the skills, patience and fine taste of their anonymous creators.

The state regalia are the true masterpieces, indeed, with the famous Monomakh's Cap, the symbol of the Czar's rule in Russia, among them. The Monomakh's Cap was the indispensable element of the coronation ceremony whereat Russian Czars were crowned for czardom. In 16th century it was popularly believed that this crown had been sent, together with other insignia of imperial power, by the Byzantine Emperor Constantine Monomakh to his grandson, Prince Vladimir of Kiev.

In 1721, Peter I announced that Russia was an Empire. Since then, the Imperial crown was a substitution for the Mono-

Pall «Our Lady's Appearance to Blessed Sergiy». Moscow. 15th century.

Monomakh's Cap. Orient. Late 13th – early 14th century.

Emperor Nicholas II's masquerade dress made according the Old Russian fashion. Moscow. 1903.

makh's Cap. One of the earliest imperial crowns, the one that belonged to Empress Anne Ioannovna, is adorned with 2,5 thousand diamonds and a huge turmalin.

The collection of old thrones is something special, too. The oldest dates back to the mid-16th century. It is believed that this parade throne, tiled with carved ivory plates, belonged to Ivan the Terrible.

The so-called Diamond Throne is lavishly decorated, too. It is all covered with golden and silver plates, intricate mosaic ornaments of turquoise and almost 900 diamonds. The throne was given to Czar Alexei Mikhailovich by Armenia's trade company.

In the days of old, the parade horse attire, carriages and especially royal processions, was something that had been taken great care of. In late 15th century, a special Stables Department was created, and its head was considered to be the second highest ranking official after the Czar. In the 17th century, among other powers, the Stables Department was responsible for 150 royal horses and 3,000 horses participating in parade processions. In the Department's workshops,

Empress Anne Ioannovna's crown. St. Petersburg. 1730–1731. Master G. Dunkel.

dozens of silversmiths and enamellists, engravers and chasers, sewers and embroiders were busy day and night. Saddles, harnesses and other pieces of horse's attire were adorned with enamel, pearls and precious stones. Chains that kept the horses together were made of silver.
In a «feather» (which was fixed on the horse's head) given to Empress Katherine II by the Turkish sultan, a huge topaz is surrounded by 1,013 small diamonds.
A great crowd of people gathered to watch the csar's train. Just imagine how impressive was the royal parade procession

The throne coated with bone plates. Western Europe. 16th century. Belonged to Ivan the Terrible.

Saddle. The Moscow Kremlin's workshops. 1637. Belonged to Czar Mikhail Feodorovich.

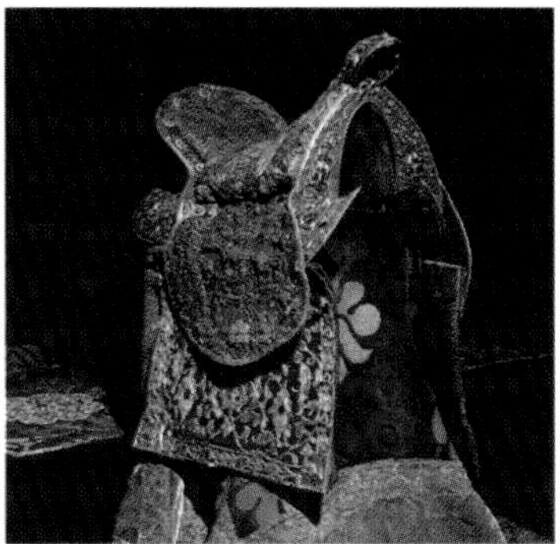

Empress Anne Ioannovna's parade carriage. St. Petersburg. 1739. Above: painting on the carriage's body.

for the onlookers standing agape!

None of the world's museums houses a collection of carriages comparable to that in the Armory Chamber. This huge exhibition gives you glimpses of the whole history of the carriage-making in the 16th–18th century. The carriage given by English King Jacob I to Boris Godunov is the oldest piece in the collection. A winter sledge looking like a railway car on runners was made by the 18th century Moscow craftsmen – it is an admirable historical item. In February 1742 the daughter of Peter I Elisabeth rode in it from St. Petersburg to attend her coronation ceremony in Moscow. The Empress-to-be was in such a hurry that she changed several hundreds horses on her long way.

The carriage presented to Elisabeth Petrovna by Ukranian getman (head of state) Kirill Razumovskiy was decorated by the then famous French royal painter Francois Buchet. Curiously enough, it has survived without having been ever repaired. One of the best examples of the Russian carriage-making is Empress Katherine II's summer coach, the gift of count Grigory Orlov.

THE DIAMOND FUND

The Diamond Fund exhibition is a unique collection of rare precious and semi-precious stones, as well s the masterpieces of jewelry.

Diadem. Ca. 1810. The rosy diamond is 13 carats.

The Orlov diamond topping the emperor's scepter.

The Shah diamond.

The Diamond Fund collection is based on the so-called crown diamonds (the royal regalia, orders and valuable jewelry articles) created in the 18–19th century. The crown collection of the Russian state was instituted by a special decree issued by Emperor Peter the Great in 1719. Since the late 18th century, the collection was kept in the Winter Palace in St. Petersburg. However, in the early days of the World War I, in 1914, the collection was transferred to Moscow. In 1922, the Russian Empire's treasures were handed over to the special Diamond Fund established in that same year. Ever since, the collection has been registered with the State Treasure Storage (Gokhran) of the Finance Ministry. For the first time ever, the Diamond Fund's wonderful collection was put on display in 1925 in the House of Unions' Column Hall in Moscow. In 1967, a permanent exhibition «The Diamond Fund» was opened in the Armory Chamber building's ground floor.

Among the exhibits, the big diamonds attract most of the visitors. Since time immemorial, the shining glow of precious stones has enchanted people who endowed them with magic powers and committed bloody crimes out of sheer wish to acquire the rare gems. Each of the diamonds displayed in the exhibition has its wonderful, if not blood-infused, story. Such is, for instance, «The Shah», an Indian diamond (88.7 carats). The Persian shah sent it to Czar Nicholas I as a compensation for the murder in Teheran of Russian Ambassador Alexander Griboyedov. Yakutian diamonds are superb, among which looms large the beautiful «Star of Yakutia» (232.1 carats) and others.

A special collection is that of the big nuggets of gold and platinum like, for instance, «The Big Triangle» (the world's largest, weightting 36.2 kg), and the fatastically shaped nuggets called «Mephistopheles», «Rabbit's Ears», «Camel».

One of the Diamond Fund's most famous exhibits is the Big Emperor's Crown virtually awash with 5,000 diamonds! The crown is topped by a dark-red spinel fixed over the diamond cross. Russian Ambassador Nikolai Spafariy purchased this rare stone in China upon the order of Czar Alexei Mikhailovich.

The crown was made in 1762 by the royal court's master jeweler Jeremy Pozier for Catherine II's coronation ceremony. Then the emperor's globe was made, too. It is a polished ball of gold with diamond bands and a diamond cross, with a huge Ceylon sapphire underneath.

The Big Emperor's Crown.

The emperor's scepter is adorned with the famous «Orlov» diamond (189.62 carats), the world's fourth largest diamond, the only one cut in the so-called 17th century Indian style. It was presented to Empress Catherine II by her former favorite Count Grigory Orlov.

The Small Emperor's Crown, as if woven of diamond laces, was made by Duval brothers for Elizavetha Alexeyevna, the wife of Czar Alexander I.

The unparalleled art of Russian and Western European jewelers is illustrated by the superb articles made of diamonds and other precious stones: sets, diadems, necklaces, broaches, earrings, pendants. You can see the broach with the purest Ceylon sapphire presented by Alexander II to his wife; a huge crystal-clear emerald in a grape-like frame of diamonds; Empress Elizavetha Alexeyevna's diadem made like an Old Russian kokoshnik, with the big rosy diamond; a broach with an olive-green chrysolite in a frame of diamonds.

The Victory order. 1950s. Master P. Kazennov.

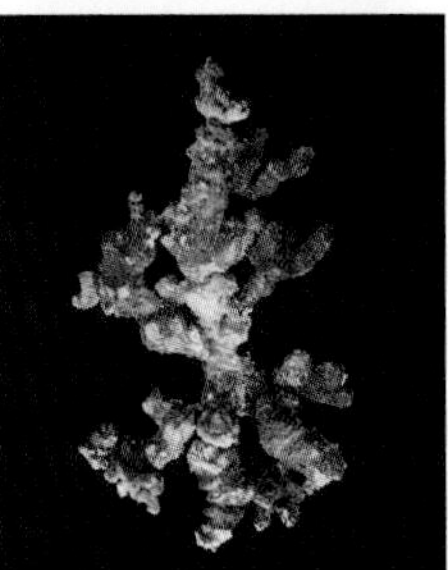

The Yolochka (Little Fir-tree) gold nugget found in the Southern Urals in 1952.

A collection of Russian orders on display in the Diamond Fund includes the regalia and chains decorated with precious stones. Along with the oldest orders of St. Andrei the First Summoned, St. Alexander Nevsky and others, you can see state decorations and regalia of the 20th century (the Marshal's Star or the Victory Order, for instance).

Of special interest are the unique masterpieces of the 20th century jewelers: «The Rose» diamond ensemble (with 1,500 diamonds), «Cosmos» (by V. Nikolayev), «The Holiday Fireworks», «The Russian Beauty» (by V. Sitnikov) and many others.

THE KREMLIN'S LARGE PALACE

A stately architectural ensemble in the Kremlin's south-western corner includes civil and church buildings constructed in the course of five centuries. The complex consists of: the Large Palace itself (built in the 19th century); the Faceted Chamber and the Holy Anteroom (built in the 15th century); the Golden Czarina's Chamber (built in the 16th century); the Terem Palace (built in the 17th century), and the palatial home churches of the 14th–17th century.

The Palace got its present-day appearance in the first half of the 19th century, when its new section with the parade façade facing the Moskva River was constructed according the design of Konstantin Ton. The main façade is 125 m long and 44 m high. There are about 700 rooms in the Palace of ca. 20,000 sq. m. Though the building is a two-storey one, you can see three rows of windows on its main façade as all the rooms upstairs are «double-lighted» (or, with two parallel rows of windows). The socle of the brick walls is tiled with gray stone, window frames are made of limestone and adorned with filigree carving and state eagles.

The 19th century Palace was erected exactly on the site where once stood the chambers of Moscow Great Princes and then the royal palaces. The survived halls and churches of the previous palatial structures were organically incorporated into the new ensemble. Before the 1917 revolution, the Palace was used as the official imperial residence in Moscow. Today, official state and major diplomatic events are held here. In the 1990s, under a large-scale and costly renovation proj-

View on the Golden Czarina's Chamber and the domes of the Terem Palace's churches.

ect, the Palace was totally refurbished with the purpose of restoring the original layout and interior décor of its parade halls.

Many palatial rooms have been safely preserved in their original look. Their furniture and interior are marked with lavish sophisticated splendor. This unique feature strikes your eye already in the Parade Vestibule where four massive columns of green granite prop the vaults. The walls are divided by eight granite pilasters with white-marble capitals.

The Private Quarters are located on the ground floor. These are the Royal Apartments, an enfilade of seven rooms with the windows facing the south. Massive pylons divide the spacious rooms into comfortable compartments decorated and furnished in different styles: baroque, rococo, classicism. Thus, the Dining-room is austerely classicist. Its walls and ceiling are reveted with artificial marble. The room's interior is given finish by a number of copied Antique statutes and wonderful porcelain vases, of which two are painted in Russian history scenes. The Empress' Sitting-room is decorated in fine rococo style. Of special interest here is a collection of Russian porcelain and a unique porcelain chandelier. The raspberry-hued Empress' Study features huge mirrors, and the so-called Boule-styled furniture lavishly encrusted with tortoise shell and bronze (the name comes from the famous 17th century French furniture-maker Andre Charles Boule). The abundance of colored marble and gilt gives an onlooker an impression of pompous luxury. The majestic fire-place in the Budoir is made of finely cut pieces of Urals malachite. The Sleeping-room looks more strict: the walls and furniture are upholstered by dark blue moire being in sharp contrast to the painted ceiling and the white marble fire-place. In the Emperor's Study, the walls are made of light ash-tree panels, the

Porcelain vase showing Kozma Minin and Dmitry Pozharskiy, a piece from the Dining-room.

The Dining-room in the Private Quarters. Pylon with a niche.

The Georgiyevskiy Hall.

A sculpture by I. Vitali.

furniture upholstered with green leather, whereas in the adjacent Emperor's Reception room the special «velvet on satin» upholstery changes its tint with the changing light.

Back in the Vestibule, you can proceed up the parade staircase and find yourself on the first floor where ceremonial halls are located: the Georgiyevskiy (St. George's), the Andreyevskiy (St. Andrew's), the Alexandrovskiy (St. Alexander's) and the Yekaterininskiy (St. Katherine's) – the names come from Russia's highest orders of military honor. The elements of the orders are incorporated in the ornaments on the arches and walls of the respective halls, and the

The fire-place clock.
The Georgiyevskiy Hall.

colors of orders are reproduced in the upholstery of the gilded furniture pieces standing in the halls.

The Palace's largest and most beautiful hall is the Georgiyevskiy. This is a sort of the Russian army's Hall of Fame, dedicated to the Order of St. Georgy established in 1769. The Hall is 61 m long, 20,5 m wide and 17,5 m high. Its northern and southern walls are adorned with high-relief images of St. George on horseback killing the Dragon with his spear (sculptor P.Klodt). On the marble plates on the walls, the names of 500 regiments and 11,000 men decorated with the Order of St. Georgy are inscribed in gold letters. Among them are Russia's outstanding men of war, Alexander Suvorov, Mikhail Kutuzov, Peter Bagration, Feodor Ushakov, Pavel Nakhimov. The vaulted ceiling is supported by 18 twisted columns topped with the sculptures by I. Vitali symbolizing the territories incorporated into Russia during the 15h–19th century. The multi-colored parquet floor made of 20 sorts of wood looks like a gigantic rug of intricate ornament.

Adjacent to the Georgieyvskiy Hall, the Vladimirskiy Hall is dedicated to the Order of St. Vladimir established in 1782 by Empress Katherine II. The Hall was built where the Boyars Ground was located in the 17th century (the Boyars Ground was a place where court men gathered in the morning waiting for the boyars to come out of the Royal Apartments and announce the Czar's new decrees and or-

View on the Kremlin's Boyars Ground. F. Alexeyev's workshop. Early 19th century.

The Vladimirskiy Hall.

ders) and it connects the old portions of the Palace with the new ones. Thus, from the Vladimirskiy Hall you can have access into the Faceted Chamber, the Golden Czarina's Chamber, the Terem Palace, and the most recent Kremlin's State Palace. The Hall is laid out like a square with cut angles. It is rather small in dimensions: it is 16 m long and wide and 18 m high. The arched walls are tiled with rose marble. Its dome-shaped vault is magnificently adorned with sculpted and gilded ornaments and insignia of the Order or St. Vladimir with its motto «Purpose. Honor. Glory». The cupola was made of empty clay pots – that is why the acoustics in the Hall is just fantastic. The cupola is topped by a lantern that lets the daylight in through its glass sides.

The Andreyevskiy Hall, the throne hall of Russian emperors, was named after the Order of St. Andrei First Summoned established in 1698. It was a place to greet highest ranking officers of the Russian army. Its walls are covered with moiré silk and adorned with the Order's insignia. Over the windows, the coats of arms of Russian regions and territories are fixed. The Hall was devoid of furniture.

The Alexandrovskiy hall is dedicated to the Order of St. Alexander Nevskiy established in 1725. The walls here were tiled with artificial rose marble, its cupola-shaped vault decorated with the Order's insignia, and in between the twisted gilded columns, the coats of arms of Russian regions and territories are fixed. In 1932–1934, both Halls were merged into a single Conference Hall (design by I. Ivanov-Shits) where the sessions of the Supreme Soviet, the highest legislative body of the Soviet Union, had been held until the early 1990s. Then, under the 1994–1996 Kremlin renovation project, the two Halls had been completely restored according to the survived blueprints and drawings.

In the first floor's western wing, you can see the enfilade of the Parade Quarters.

Medallion with Emperor Nicholas I's monogram in the Andreyevskiy Hall.

The Andreyevskiy Hall.

Above: the Alexandrovskiy Hall.

Below: the Yekaterininskiy Hall.

Doors with the Order's insignia in the Yekaterininskiy Hall.

The light-silvery Yekaterininskiy Hall, once was used as the Empress' reception room. Its name comes from the Order of St. Katherine, established by Peter I in 1714, the only one that was dedicated to the female saint and awarded to women. The walls and doors of the Hall are adorned with the Order's insignia and motto: «For Love and Motherland». The key attractions here are massive pylons with pilasters adorned with the mosaic ornament made of malachite

The Sitting-room's painting. Detail.

pieces and the wonderful parquet floor of multi-color panels.

The Parade Sitting-room is a lavishly furnished spacious room used to greet distinguished guests. Its vaulted ceiling is painted in elegant vegetation ornaments, the walls and the furniture upholstered by gold-and-green brocade. The Boule-styled furniture is encrusted with tortoise shell mother of pearl, bronze and different kinds of wood. The interior décor is supplemented by china chandeliers made by Russian craftsmen in the Japanese and Chinese manner. The fire-place made of Carrara white marble features the old French clock.

The adjacent Parade Sleeping-room is rather small and has an alcove with monolith columns of gray-green marble. The fire-place is coated with green-blue jasper, which is in sharply contrast with the walls' upholstery of bright-raspberry tint. The Parade Quarters ends in the Nut Wardrobe where the walls and the ceiling are coated with nut-tree panels.

The Large Palace's true gem is the Faceted Chamber, Moscow's oldest civil building, the former throne hall of Moscow Great Princes and Czars. According to the chronicle, in the late 15th century, «there was founded a stone and brick chamber» for Great Prince Ivan III. Over time, of the Great

The Faceted Chamber.

The Holy Anteroom's portal.

The fresco on the Faceted Chamber's vaulted ceiling. Detail.

The Faceted Chamber's eastern wall-painting. Detail. Left to right: Princes Ryurik, Igor, Svyatoslav Igorevich.

Prince's ancient palace only the stone cube of the Faceted Chamber has been preserved, the ceremonial hall built in 1487– 1491 under the supervision of Italian architects Marco Ruffo and Pietro Antonio Solari. It acquired its name after its Oriental-style façade coated with faceted white-stone plates. Old Russian and Italian traditions were combined in the Chamber's architectural design. Eighteen windows arranged in two rows let daylight in. After it was restored after the 1648 fire, the Chamber's interior was marked with extraordinary magnificence and splendor. Back then, the windows were widened, and white-stone frames adorned with baroque carving were added.

In its time, the Faceted Chamber was the largest building in the Russian capital city – 495 sq. m. The square-shaped hall was 9 m high. Its cross-shaped vaults are propped by a four-faceted pole. You can enter into the Chamber via the white-stone gilded carved portal dating back to the 15th–17th century. The carved ornament resembles that on the central pole inside the Chamber. Gilded dolphins, beasts and birds are depicted on each facet.

For the first time, the Chamber's walls were painted in the late 16th century, but the original frescoes have not survived. The present-day frescoes were created in 1882 by Belousov brothers, the artists from the town of Palekh, who relied on the descriptions made

The Faceted Chamber's eastern wall.

The pole in the middle of the Faceted Chamber.

The Faceted Chamber's portal.

by Simon Ushakov, the famous 17th century icon-maker. The wall-painting's key idea was the celebration of the Czar's power. Of special interest are the frescoes on the eastern wall and a portion of the southern wall where the Czar's throne once stood. Here, the painters used the plot of the 17th century «Story of the Princes of Vladimir» that reflected the idea of continuity of power from Byzantium and even Rome down to Moscow Princes. By the way, in the 15th–17th century, widely spread was the political myth «Moscow as the Third Rome» whereby Russian monarchs were declared the successors of Roman and Byzantine emperors. Thus, one fresco shows the first princes of the Ryurik dynasty who were, according to a legend, descendants of Roman Emperor August Octavian. You can see in the frescoes Kiev Prince Vladimir with his 12 sons, Prince Vladimir II Monomakh, Czars Feodor Ioannovich, and Boris Godunov, episodes from the Biblical parables about Joseph in slavery, about the just and unjust judgment. 24 portraits of Russian rulers are painted on the slopes of the windows.

Adjacent to the Faceted Chamber is the Red Porch with the staircase leading into the Holy Anteroom, the reception-room where guests were sitting and waiting to be received by the Czar (the Red staircase was restored in the 1990s). The Holy Anteroom's key attraction is the six carved white-stone portals adorned with ornaments and gilt (the four of them made in the 19th century). The wall

The supreme dinner in the Faceted Chamber. From the book «Holy Coronation of Sovereign Emperor Alexander III». 1883.

paintings based on the Biblical and historical plots were made by F. Zavyalov in the 19th century.

The Faceted Chamber was a place to celebrate the major state events in Old Russia, to hold official ceremonies like the regional councils and boyar Duma, to receive foreign ambassadors. Here, in 1552 Czar Ivan the Terrible celebrated his conquest of Kazan; in 1654, the decision on Ukraine's reunion with Russia was made; in 1672, Czar Alexei Mikhailovich marked the birth of his son Peter, and in 1709 Czar Peter celebrated his victory in the Battle of Poltava. During sparkling royal reception parties, the Chamber's floor would be covered by magnificent Persian carpets, a postavets, a high stepped table full of precious silverware, was put near the central pole. At present, the Faceted Chamber is still a special place for parade ceremonies and major state events.

The Golden Czarina's Chamber. The south-eastern vault's painting.

The Golden Czarina's Chamber, rather small in size, located on a high arched podklet (ground floor) near the Faceted Chamber, was built in the 16th century and was used as Russian Czarinas' reception room. Its gateway is a gilded white-stone portal covered with a web of vegetation ornaments. The Golden Czarina's Chamber looks more austere and less official than the Faceted Chamber. Its original interior was changed after a new palatial church, the Verkhospasskiy Cathedral, was built over it in 1636. New stone arches were fixed inside the Chamber, whereas the vaults were reinforced with iron beams. It was given its name in the 16th century after its elegant wall-painting against the golden background. Under a restoration project in 1978–1980, the 17th century wall-painting was recovered that was based on the stories about the lives of Orthodox Princesses and Czarinas, Olga, Yelena, Irina, and Theodora, the wife of Byzantine Emperor Pheophil, and Dinara, the queen of Georgia. In front of the Czarina's Chamber, there is the so-called Dwellers Chamber – an anteroom where «dwellers» (the Palace's guards and servants) were always present.

In 1635–1636, on the site where the old palace (khoromy) of Prince Vassiliy III and Ivan the Terrible once stood, the new Terem Palace was built for Mikhail Feodorovich, the first czar in the Romanov dynasty. The construction project was supervised by the outstanding Russian architects Antipa Konstantinov, Trefil Sharutin, Bazhen Ogurtsov and Larion Ushakov. The new rooms were erected over the two stories of the 15th–16th century structure that subsequently were used as storage rooms and cellars. The beautiful, painted in bright colors, five-story palace, with its white-stone decorative carve-work, glazed and tiled cornices, sharp-edged roofs and towers is the real masterpiece of the Russian architecture. Its podklIets (ground floor rooms) were used as cellars, its second and third story housed workshops where dozens of craftsmen made and kept royal attire; also, there were guest rooms up there. The fourth story housed the Czar's pri-

The Terem Palace's southern façade.

The Golden Grille. Fragment.

A passageway to the Terem Palace's gallery.

vate apartments (the Czarina had her separate, wooden, rooms). The upper floor was the so-called Zolotoy teremok (golden-topped little tower), or Stone Attic, with painted roof and an open walking space – gulbishche, with the high round Watchtower. The gulbishche was surrounded by a parapet with the wrought-iron grille. The Zolotoy Teremok was a place where Czareviches lived.

From Cathedral Square to the parade rooms of the Terem Palace, from the upper Golden Porch to the lower Boyars Ground, led a carved staircase. When the Large Palace was under construction in the first half of the 19th century, the upper porch and ground in front of it was incorporated in the new palatial ensemble, and an arch was built over it. The arch of the Golden Porch was adorned with the decorative lion's head. So, the gateway to the Palace is guarded by ominous stone lions standing on hind legs. Under a 1960s renovation project, the Porch's ancient painting was recovered and the 17th century Golden Grille in front of it was completely restored.

The royal apartments on the fourth floor consist of five rooms almost alike in size, whose interior is an example of the early 17th century affluent home. In its layout the rooms reproduce an ordinary Russian izba (village house) with three windows on its façade; however, they were decorated in the most luxurious way. Colored mica was inserted in the windows having white-stone carved frames, the floor was made of oak «bricks» and covered with green

The Terem Palace's Golden Porch. 17th century.

The Terem Palace's Verkhospasskaya Ground. Master Belogolovov. 1852.

The tiled stove in the Terem Palace's Throne Chamber.

or red broadcloth. On special days, expensive carpets were laid. The first room, Anteroom or Refectory, had painted vaults and the beautiful tiled stoves. Benches covered with velvet were an indispensable element of the interior. In the room, boyars and Duma clerks gathered here in this room waiting for the Czar's appearance, sometimes they ate in there. The second room, the Gathering, or Duma, Chamber, the Czar held meetings with his boyars. The next room is the Throne (Prestolnaya) Chamber, or the Czar's Study. Its walls are painted in golden-red hues and adorned with gilded coats of arms of Russian regions. The velvet-upholstered Czar's seat is in the corner.

Adjacent to the Throne Chamber room is called the Sleeping-room, though its initial purpose is unknown. In the middle of the room, a carved 19th century bed under a canopy stands. The walls and the vaulted ceiling are painted in complicated ornamental designs. The room was heated by the tiled stove restored in the 19th century according to the old drawings. Lastly, right behind the Sleeping-room is a small Praying-

The Czar's Study in the Terem Palace. Drawing by Shadurskiy. 1851.

The Church of Glorious Sunday's iconostasis. Fragment.

room, with a beautiful carved iconostasis adorned with the gilded grapevine ornament. This iconostasis features the 17th–18th century icons. In 1812 Napoleon's soldiers pillaged the Terem Palace, the ancient furniture and rare fabrics were stolen, wall painting was badly damaged. Over the last two centuries, the Palace was more than once under renovation. The present-day panting was made in 1836 by Timofei Kiselev according to the sketches by Feodor Solntsev. The Palace was under restoration in the mid-20th century, too. In spite of numerous changes, the Terem Palace has been preserved in almost original look.

When standing on Cathedral Square and admiring the majestic cathedrals around you, you must have taken notice, to the left of the Church of Laying Our Lady's Robe, of 11 filigree crosses over the golden onion-shaped cupolas standing on high tiled drums. These are the domes of the churches of the Kremlin's Large Palace that were used as private chapels by the members of the royal family. Besides making the regular prayers in the morn-

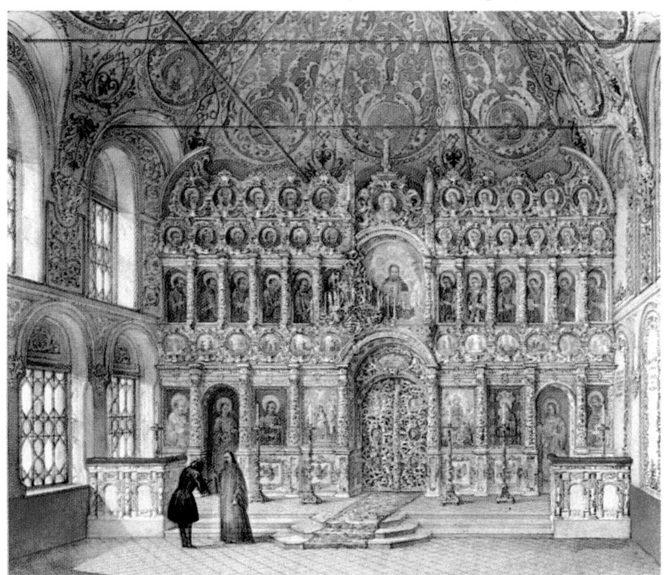

The Church of Glorious Sunday in the Moscow Kremlin. Drawing by P. Gerasimov. Mid-19th century.

ing and before going to bed in those private chapels, the Czar and the royal family visited the palatial churches twice a day.

The oldest church among those survived is the Church of Our Lady's Nativity. This stone cathedral was built in 1393 on the order of Great Princess Yevdokia, the wife of Dmitry Donskoi (instead of the yet older wooden Church of Lazarus' Resurrection) . In 1395, the new church was painted by Pheophan the Greek. In 1515, Italian architect Aleviz Noviy overbuilt another church that was also named the Church of Our Lady's Nativity, whereas the lower one was re-consecrated and re-named the Church of Lazarus' Resurrection. The Nativity Church has been preserved in its 17th century version.

The Nativity Cathedral was the Czarinas' home church. Services were held in it on Sundays and major church holidays. The lower white-stone Church of Lazarus' Resurrection was then hidden under subsequently constructed rooms, and was utterly forgotten. In 1837, when the Large Palace construction project was under way, builders found an obscure room with fragments of wall-painting. Upon Emperor Nicholas I's order, the ancient church was reconstructed.

In 1635–1636, Czar Mikhail Feodorovich's main home church was built and consecrated in the name of Veronica, and named the Savior Behind the Golden Grille. The Terem Palace's Golden Porch and the Cathedral were separated by a beautiful copper grille. Oit was gilded and painted in intricate fairy-tale designs and was given the name Golden. The cathedral was also called Verkhospasskiy (Upper Savior's), as it was built on the Palace's third floor, or, as they used to say in the days of old, «in the Czar's anteroom». The Cathedral was erected

Icon «Savior in the Crown of Thorns». 1682. From the Church of Crucifixion's iconostasis.

The Verkhospasskiy Cathedral's iconostasis. 17th–19th century.

by renowned Russian builders Trofim Sharutin, Bazhen Ogurtsov, Antipa Konstantinov and Larion Ushakov, was eventually more than once reconstructed.

In 1680–1681, on the Terem Palace's third floor, over the St. Katherine's Church, to the north of the Verkhospasskiy Cathedral, another home church was built, the Church of the Glorious Sunday. The Cathedral's true treasure is the superb iconostasis, an example of the early Moscow baroque. The iconostasis was made by a team of outstanding Kremlin's masters: Simon Ushakov, Sergei Rozhnov, Feodor Zubov, Ivan Saltanov and others.

The St. Katherine's Church's iconostasis. Fragment.

An icon from the Church of Our Lady's Nativity's refectory.

In 1681, a small home Church of the Crucifixion was built on the Terem Palace's fourth floor. Its unique iconostasis was made by the gifted royal icon-painter Vassiliy Poznanskiy. He was the first to use in his art the appliqué technique: he painted the saints' faces in oil on canvas, whereas the garments, the background and other elements of his compositions were made of pieces of foreign silk glued on canvas.

The St. Katherine Church consecrated in the name of martyr saint Katherine was built in 1627–1628 on the Terem Palace's second floor, over the Church of the Glorious Sunday, by English architect John Taller, especially for czarinas and czarevnas. The St. Katherine Church standing on the same site was first mentioned in 1587. This martyr saint Czarina was the most revered by the royal family. In the 19th century, the Church was reconstructed.

A HISTORY OF THE MOSCOW KREMLIN. BRIEF CHRONOLOGY

1147 The Moscow Kremlin is first mentioned in the chronicle. This year is considered the beginning of Moscow's history

1156 Upon Prince Yuri Dolgorukiy's order, his men erected on the Borovitskiy Hill a protective stockade with the wooden fence around the settlement

1325 After Metropolitan of Kiev and All Russia Peter moved to Moscow from Vladimir, the Kremlin comes to be the official center of the Russian Orthodox Church

1339–1340 Ivan Kalita surrounded the Kremlin with solid oak walls of 2 to 6 m thick and up to 7 m high. Stone churches are being built in the Kremlin

1367–1368 Moscow Prince Dmitry Ivanovich (Donskoy) built a new fortress of white stone. The white-stone Kremlin had stood for 100 years

The second half of the 14th century. The Chudov Monastery and the Voznesenskiy Nunnery are founded near the Frolovskaya (now Spasskaya) Tower. Both had existed until the 1930s.

The second half of the 15th century. By 1480, Old Russia was finally liberated from the Mongol-Tartar yoke. In the time of Great Prince Ivan III Moscow comes to be the capital city of the united Russian principalities. A massive construction project supervised by Italian architects is launched in the Kremlin

1475–1479 The Assumption Cathedral is erected on Cathedral Square, the Moscow Russia's main cathedral, the Metropolitans and Patriarchs' burial place

1484–1489 Pskov's builders construct the Moscow Princes' home church, the Annunciation Cathedral and a small one-domed Church of Laying Our Lady's Holy Robe. In between the Annunciation and Assumption Cathedrals, the Faceted Chamber, Moscow's Great Princes' reception hall, is begun to be erected

1485 A new redbrick fortress is begun to be constructed. The fortress had 18 towers; its walls were 5 to 19 m high and 3.5 to 6.5 m thick. The construction project lasted for 10 years

1505–1508 The Archangels' Cathedral, the Great Princes and, later, Czars' necropolis is constructed on Cathedral Square, together with the Ivan the Great Bell-tower. Originally, the Bell-tower was three-tiered; subsequently, two more tiers were added, and until the 19th century, it was Moscow's tallest building

1534–1538 A new circle of defensive walls – Kitay-Gorod (Chinatown). From the southern approach, the Kitay-Gorod walls were attached to the Kremlin's wall near the Beklemishchevskaya Tower. From the northern approach, the new walls were attached to the Kremlin's wall near the Arsenalnaya corner-tower.

17th century In the early years of this century, the Kremlin was conquered and looted by Polish invaders. After the invaders were driven out, Mikhail Feodorovich was elected Czar to be the first in the Romanov dynasty that ruled in Russia for over three centuries

1635–1636 Russian builders construct the Terem Palace and home churches, the parade royal residence

1651–1652 Near the Komendantskaya Tower, a palace was built for Czar Alexei Mikhailovich's son-in-law, nobleman Miloslavskiy, which was later called the Fun Palace. After the nobleman died, the Palace was given over to the royal treasury

1652–1656 Patriarch Nikon has his new residence erected, the Patriarch's Palace with the Twelve Apostles' Church. The buildings give finish to the Cathedral Square's ensemble

1702 A new Arsenal, the weaponry, ammunition and Russian war trophies storage, is built

The first quarter of the 18th century. In 1703, Czar Peter I abolishes Patriarchate in Russia, and in 1712 makes St. Petersburg the capital city of the Russian Empire. However, key state events are still held in the Kremlin's cathedrals

1776–1787 The Senate is built near the Arsenal

1812 Napoleon's army takes Moscow. Many Kremlin's buildings were badly damaged. After the French troops were driven out, a massive restoration project was launched in the Kremlin. In 1817–1823, a huge park – later called Alexandrov Gardens – was created outside the Kremlin

1839–1849 In the southwestern corner, the Kremlin's Large Palace is built. The old buildings and churches were incorporated in this cyclopic ensemble that came to Moscow's royal residence and a place to hold official events

1844–1851 In between the Kremlin's Large Palace and the Borovitskaya Tower, the Armory Chamber museum is built. It houses exhibits of Russian and foreign armaments and unique pieces of applied art of the 4–20th century

1918 After the October 1917 Revolution, Moscow once again becomes Russia's capital city. The Kremlin is the government's official residence. It remained closed to the public until 1955

1932–1934 The old monastery and the nunnery near the Spasskaya Tower are dismantled, and a building for Red Commander's School (later, the Presidium of the Supreme Soviet building) is erected instead

1959–1961 The Palace of Congresses (later, the Kremlin's State Palace), Moscow's biggest public building, is built

Late 20th – early 21st century. After the USSR ceased to exist, Moscow becomes the capital of the Russian Federation, and the Kremlin, the official residence of the Russian President. A large-scale Kremlin renovation project is completed. On major church holidays, Patriarch of Moscow and All Russia conducts services in the Kremlin's cathedrals

9
8
10
7
6
5
4
M
7
3
42
2
43
1
28

M
11
13
15
12
18
14
38
40
16
37
35
19
17
33
20
32
34
29
45
36
21
31
6
30
22
23
44
24
25
26
27

A GUIDE

MOSCOW KREMLIN

Managing editor
Lydia Zakharova

Translator
Oleg Alyakrinsky

Production editor
Galina Popova

ART-COURIER

Издание на английском языке

Тираж 10 000 экз.

Printed in Italy

This guidebook will be a helpful company during your walks inside the Moscow Kremlin. The ancient fortress on the Borovitskiy Hill over the Moskva River is the most famous tourist attraction in the Russian capital. The history of the Kremlin, a political, spiritual and cultural center of the nation, is imprinted in its stately walls and towers, its golden-domed cathedrals and churches, its majestic and elegant palaces. Surely, getting to know the unique architectural monuments of the Moscow Kremlin will be one of the most vivid impressions in your life.